STO

A GUIDE TO FINANCIAL INSTITUTIONS

Charles R. Geisst
Manhattan College, Riverdale, New York

St. Martin's Press   New York

© Charles R. Geisst, 1988

All rights reserved. For information, write:
Scholarly & Reference Division,
St. Martin's Press, Inc., 175 Fifth Avenue, New York, NY 10010

First published in the United States of America in 1988

Printed in Hong Kong

ISBN 0–312–01132–6 (cloth)
ISBN 0–312–01133–4 (pbk)

Library of Congress Cataloging-in-Publication Data
Geisst, Charles R.
A guide to financial institutions.
"A companion volume to the same author's A
guide to the financial markets"—Jacket.
Includes bibliographies and index.
1. Financial institutions—United States.
2. Financial institutions—Great Britain.
3. Financial institutions, International.   I. Title.
HG185.U6G45   1988   332.1   87–13047
ISBN 0–312–01132–6
ISBN 0–312–01133–4 (pbk.)

For Margaret the Elder

Contents

List of Tables

Acknowledgements

The author is grateful to many colleagues, both in the investment banking world and later in academia, whose comments
and continual discussion helped in the development of this
book. During the later stages of writing, I was also aided
immeasurably by attending the twenty-sixth Central Banking
Seminar held at the Federal Reserve Bank of New York. While
the focal point of this book is primarily commercial institutions, this particular seminar helped to bring the many interre-
lationships between financial institutions into better perspective. And finally, a word of thanks to Aileen Kelly, who helped
edit the manuscript.

CHARLES R. GEISST

Introduction

In the late 1970s and early 1980s, the major topic of discussion within and among financial institutions was high interest rates, especially those in the United States, and the various problems they created. When worldwide rates did begin to subside, the discussion shifted to institutional changes that were becoming necessary as a result of the changes in the financial climate of the previous decade. The net result has been a significant change in the attitudes of regulatory authorities that direct financial institutions as well as structural changes in the institutions themselves.

The methodological problem that immediately presents itself to anyone interested in these changes is that they are essentially international in character. It is no longer possible to classify developments in the American or British banking industries as purely domestic in nature. The free flow of capital between the major international capital centres, prompted by foreign exchange and real rate of return motives, has made what were once international counterparts now international competitors in the quest for commercial or investment banking fees. While it may still be a bit early to draw conclusions concerning the end effect of these multitudinous institutional changes this book does attempt to begin its discussion of financial institutions with the international sector.

This present volume is intended to be a companion volume to this same author's *A Guide to the Financial Markets*, first published by Macmillan and St. Martin's in 1982. The treatment of the subject matter also follows the same *modus operandi*. This volume is intended to be an introduction to the topic; it does not attempt nor pretend to cover it exhaustively. Therefore, readers more accustomed to textbook presentations will find a distinct lack of familiar pedagological devices such as the

T-account or other accounting considerations when discussing the basic mechanics of banking or of money creation. But it should not be implied that textbook presentations are not of value; they have, however, been done so many times before that this author has decided to rely only upon prose given the introductory nature of the book.

Although the content of this book is intended to be Anglo-American, the latter institutions tend to take precedence over the former in many examples. The reasons for this are purely practical, given the size and breadth of American financial institutions. Nevertheless, many of the practices and procedures of commercial banking, investment banking, and building associations are very similar in both countries and general descriptions, with obvious qualifications, can be made without constantly referring to one country or the other. The historical reasons for this similarity are fairly complex but if one generalisation may be permitted it would have to do with the British ability to invent and the American ability to develop. After a century and a half of such cross-fertilisation, it becomes increasingly obvious that many original British financial practices have become Americanised, developed further, and exported back to Britain through the new, fast-developing international marketplace.

Of course, this Anglo-American exchange of ideas and practices is certainly not new. As early as the latter part of the eighteenth century, Samuel Slater imported the idea of the spinning jenny into the United States and successfully set up shop in Rhode Island, spinning cotton yarns which, until that time, had been a cherished and closely-guarded British invention. The same process occurs today but the products involved probably would bewilder Mr Slater. The British banking practice of lending on an adjustable, or floating, basis has been incorporated by American investment banks into securities called floating rate notes. Similarly, American commercial banks have developed merchant banking units in order to compete for fee income (non-deposit/lending income). Their name is an explicit reference to the group of British institutions performing the same function, only having done so for the last two hundred years.

Developments in the early and mid 1980s have proceeded at an almost staggering pace. The de-regulation of the American banking industry has seen interest rate ceilings on deposit accounts crumble, commercial banks expand by buying up other commercial banks and depository institutions across state lines, and the expansion of insurance companies into other lines of financial services, not to mention the influx of foreign banks into the American brokerage business. In Britain, foreign institutions have bought up British brokerage houses and become dealers in UK government securities, once the traditional preserve of British firms. Similarly, pressure from other stock exchanges has caused the London Stock Exchange to abandon its old commission structure, while the increasing pressure from the international marketplace has led to several large proposed bank mergers.

All of these changes, and the interest rate and other economic conditions that prompted them, have spawned a new financial services industry quite different from the one preceding it. Rationalisation, or centralisation, has become the byword as many large, full-service financial institutions have replaced smaller, single function institutions. Both international and domestic competitive pressures have become so great that the small, less capitalised firms find themselves at a distinct disadvantage to the larger offering their services on a global scale. But whether or not this trend succeeds in the long run depends upon the individual, who has for decades been accustomed to shopping for his financial services on a shop by shop basis rather than visiting a financial superstore offering all sorts of services and products under one roof. Whether he is willing to purchase insurance, personal pension plans, equities and bonds, and perhaps even consumer goods, from the same institution remains to be seen.

While this book has been written in such an environment, it still seeks to stress the basics of the major financial institutions rather than emphasise innovation. 'Revolutions' as such are difficult periods in which to write although the present 'financial services revolution' appears to be more structural than functional. Commercial banking will still be practised by commercial banks and investment banking will still be practised by investment banks. Their ownership may change significantly as time goes on but the basic functions they perform will probably remain the same.

1 International Financial Institutions

At the very heart of the international financial system are several institutions whose main purpose is to aid in the international payments mechanism. Because of their diverse natures, these entities are difficult to categorise but they do nevertheless share common traits. In a structural sense, their common denominator is a transnational character that spans national boundaries.

Occasionally, the term 'supranational' is used to describe such institutions. However, this is not a correct generic term, for supranational is a name used to describe the second sort of institution described here: those organisations whose everyday business is to aid international or regional development of, or on behalf of, their member states. Sometimes, these institutions themselves are considered sovereign. But supranational is not an appropriate term to describe those two institutions at the very top of the system – the Bank for International Settlements and the International Monetary Fund.

As will be seen in this and later chapters, the premier financial institution in any national economy is that which performs the ultimate banking function – that of lender of last resort. Usually, this function is reserved for the central bank of a country to which other financial institutions can turn for assistance in times of need. During the international financial crisis that developed in the early 1980s, however, several financial institutions stepped into the natural breach that exists in the international system so that some Third World debt repayments and re-schedulings could be facilitated without damaging the structure and confidence of the international financial community as such. The reason that this effort was concerted was simple: the international system as it is presently constituted does not have an original lender of last resort. Although this system is composed of diverse institutions, they are not all official organisations with clearly defined cross-national functions. The international network of commercial banks and, to a lesser extent, investment banks that regularly transact business such as foreign exchange dealings, security issues, and international payments, generally also plays a crucial role in international trade. Without these banks, the larger official institutions would have to play a much larger role than they do currently. However, in structural terms, the official institutions are those facilitating the efficiency of the system as such and deal with the larger problems posed by international trade and trade-related problems.

In many ways, the international financial system and the institutions dominating it have much in common with institutions of public international law, if only by analogy. Critics of international political institutions often contend that they actually have little real effect other than to serve as international debating bodies that otherwise pack little, if any, coercive power. Given that there is no official lender of last resort in international terms or any central set of regulations or laws governing sovereign debt, some critics have contended that the system is more nomenclature than reality. However, in practical terms, experience has shown that the system has developed well over the last several decades, especially since the end of the Second World War. It was in the financial chaos caused by the war and its aftermath that the idea of modern international financial institutions was implemented. The idea itself was somewhat older, having been attempted after the First World War but it crumbled during the intervening years.

BRIEF HISTORY OF INTERNATIONAL FINANCIAL INSTITUTIONS

The need for a banking institution that could transcend the limitations of both central banks and the larger internationally-oriented commercial banks was felt after the First World War, especially after it became obvious that a return to the pre-war gold standard was impractical. But it was not until 1930 that the concept became reality with the establishment of the Bank for International Settlements (BIS). The BIS was established in order to expedite German war reparations by reducing and commercialising German payments.

The BIS was established in Basle on 17 May 1930 with a hybrid legal structure. Organisationally, it was structured as a limited company with its members holding capital shares; its members being sovereign states. Legally, its personality is that of an international organisation created by the Hague convention of 1930, meaning that its legal character is a document of international law rather than Swiss law. Although it is a bank, it is not subject to Swiss federal law governing banks. Neither is it subject to Swiss company law; its shareholders are actually the central banks of its members rather than individuals or companies.

Simply, the BIS is the central bankers' bank. Its clients (also its shareholders) are associated central banks; it does not deal with the commercial banking community except in the case of investments for its own portfolio. Over eighty central banks deal with the BIS on a day-to-day basis in order to manage their reserves. In this respect, it buys and sells currencies, depending upon demand from its clients. According to the Bank itself, almost 10 per cent of world foreign exchange reserves are managed through its facilities.

Functioning as a central bank in this respect, the BIS is at the very heart of the international system in much the same way the Federal Reserve is at the heart of the American financial system or the Bank of England is in Britain. Its other major functions include being a forum for international monetary cooperation, acting as agent in certain international agreements, and providing international banking research and statistical services. But one major central banking function, that of controlling currency or money supply, is not carried out. This function, if actually appropriate in the international arena, is carried out in a sense by the other central, public financial institution, the International Monetary Fund, or IMF.

While the BIS successfully helps central banks manage their reserves and performs trustee functions for government loans, the aftermath of the Second World War helped create a new class of financial institutions whose major function was to aid in the allocation of monetary reserves on a regional and worldwide basis. The BIS performed, and still performs, an international management function but events in the post-war era signalled a new period in the international monetary order which demanded new types of institutions able to cope with rapidly changing financial events on a global scale.

During the Second World War, currency stability was seriously undermined by balance of payments disequilibria among the major trading nations. As a result, the United Nations Monetary and Financial Conference held in Bretton Woods, New Hampshire, in 1944 created two new organisations designed, in different ways, to cope with the attendant problems – the IMF and the International Bank for Reconstruction and Development (World Bank). In general terms, both were able to complement the BIS's activities on a grand scale that had ironically been envisioned at the Hague Conference of 1930 but never fully implemented.

The IMF's principles sound similar in theory to those of the BIS in that both institutions seek to promote international financial cooperation, facilitate payments, and promote balanced growth in trade. Where they differ is in the IMF's ability to make temporary financial resources available to members in order to enable them to correct payment imbalances without resorting to potentially destructive actions such as competitive currency depreciation, imposing exchange controls, or resorting to trade protectionism.

Also of primary importance is the IMF's ability to promote exchange rate stability. An example of this principle and how it operates in practice can be found in the monetary history of the post-war period. Originally, members of the IMF were required to establish what was known as a 'par value' for their currencies in gold terms through the US dollar as of 1944 and thereafter maintain the market rate of their respective currencies within a margin of one per cent on either side of that value. This par value could only be changed if the member proposed it after consulting with the IMF. This system worked adequately for about ten years because many countries still protected their currencies through exchange controls and restrictive practices as an aftermath of war. Gradually, as many countries improved their balance of payments positions after the war, the IMF began to take new monetary initiatives.

In 1969, the IMF created the Special Drawing Right (SDR)

which was to become a new financial asset used to supplement foreign exchange reserves of its members. But before the SDR could receive widespread attention, as it eventually did in the 1970s, several international financial incidents occurred helping to destroy the old par value system. Between 1967 and 1971, several currency devaluations and revaluations occurred, aggravating exchange rate pressures. Finally, in August 1971, the United States suspended the convertibility of the dollar into gold and a new pattern of exchange rates with wider bands of divergence was agreed upon. From December 1971 a band of ±2.25 per cent was established for all major currencies, except the Canadian dollar.

This new regime proved short-lived and in February 1973 the parity system effectively terminated when the US devalued the dollar by 10 per cent, closing the foreign exchange markets for two and a half weeks. When the markets reopened, the Japanese yen and the six currencies of the (then) European Economic Community were allowed to float freely against the dollar.

Floating exchange rates have been the order of the day since that time. Under such conditions, currencies are valued purely on a supply and demand basis; that is, the market values each without a particular reference point such as par value. But this is not to imply that all currencies have independent value *vis-à-vis* others. Regional currency alignments still exist either officially or unofficially and not all currencies float freely against others. Yet it was the tumultuous monetary history of the 1974–80 period that gave the SDR an increasing role in international financial transactions nevertheless.

Following IMF guidelines, the SDR is an artificial currency, calculated on a weighted basis of the world's major trading currencies. Originally, it was used purely as a central bank reserve asset and could be created or cancelled only by the IMF. But during the latter 1970s, it also became used in some commercial transactions. In most instances, the rationale behind its use was the same: it was utilised by those who wanted to protect their assets against US dollar depreciation.

The mid to late 1970s saw the US dollar under attack on the foreign exchange markets, usually in favour of the Deutschemark, Japanese yen, sterling and, to a lesser extent, the Dutch guilder. Since most central banks held a large proportion of their reserves in dollars, a drop in its market value could only lead to a re-evaluation of the foreign reserves held. For instance, a central bank may have held 75 per cent of its reserves, say $10 billion, in dollars with the balance being diversified into the other major currencies. Usually the portfolio mix depended upon the nature of the country's trade patterns plus other demographic factors such as its physical location, size, and preference of its citizens for foreign denominated assets.

If the dollar was to depreciate some 10 per cent against the other currencies, a central bank would be in a positon of writing down $750 million from its reserves. Whether it would recover some of the loss from the balance of its portfolio would depend upon the performance of the other currencies but in this simple example even if the others (the balance, $2.5 billion) appreciated by 10 per cent, its coffers would still be $500 million short of the original value due to the heavy reliance on the dollar originally. Because of its weighting, the SDR helped offset this problem.

The current composition of the SDR is shown in Table 1.1. While the artificial currency did not become a substitute for holding dollars it nevertheless gave central banks opting for it protection against downward fluctuations. As can be seen, the weight of the dollar in the basket is substantially less than the figure used in the example above.

Obviously, the SDR affords downside protection against a dollar slide but it will still be worth less if the dollar should appreciate, as it did in the early 1980s. And in a purely commercial sense, it is also somewhat limited by the number of financial assets it can be invested in since, unlike the dollar, no

TABLE 1.1 Composition of the Special Drawing Right

Currency	%
US dollar	42
Deutschemark	19
Sterling	13
French franc	13
Japanese yen	13
total	100

SOURCE: IMF *Survey*

well developed capital market exists for commercially created SDRs.[1]

While the impact of the SDR upon the international financial system may not be known for some time, it is nevertheless fair to say that it has helped supplant some of the hard European currencies as the second reserve asset held by some central banks, especially since the decline of sterling, both in value and popularity. But perhaps one of the IMF's most notable achievements, besides the creation of the basket currency, was in aiding Third World debt rescheduling in the 1980s.

As mentioned earlier, the major problem encountered when considering the international financial system as a whole is that there is no official lender of last resort, due to political and financial balkanisation. This vacuum in the system has put tremendous pressure upon both the BIS and the IMF as well as upon the Federal Reserve System of the United States whose member commercial banks have been the primary lenders of funds (mainly US dollars) to the developing world in the wake of the OPEC price rises of the 1970s and the subsequent dollar surplus balances that wound their way through the international banking system. While commercial banks are responsible for writing the loans, they have, in most cases, looked for guidance to those institutions at the top of the system in working out amicable, if not profitable, solutions when the ability to repay those loans became doubtful.

During the first Mexican repayment crisis, beginning in the autumn of 1982, an effective restructuring of that country's debt schedule was negotiated with the IMF and the BIS both playing a central role in negotiations. And both intitutions also extended credit to Mexico in the form of loans in order to help it ward off default on its nearest payments outstanding. Although the amounts extended were relatively small in relation to Mexico's total debt outstanding (an estimated $90 billion), the ability to help the commercial banks in time of crisis illustrated the crucial role these institutions can play in this amorphous system. Without the advice of the IMF particularly and the readiness to advance some funds, the actual rescheduling would probably have taken longer and had a more serious impact upon commercial banks' balance sheets and stock market values.

In addition to the accomplishments listed briefly above, the

IMF has also developed loan arrangements that can be made with member states in order to help offset structural problems in their balance of payments. These types of loans are made in SDRs, the official currency of the Fund, and enable a member country to borrow without resorting to commercial borrowing at higher interest rates.

Although both the IMF and the BIS are somewhat limited in what they are able to accomplish, their activities are sometimes duplicated by another set of international institutions that operate on a regional, rather than on a global, basis. When the activities of these institutions is combined, the net effect can be quite considerable.

SUPRANATIONAL INSTITUTIONS AND DEVELOPMENT BANKS

During the immediate post-war period, the need for economic cooperation and development became so acute that former antagonists put aside past differences and entered into mutual economic agreements that would eventually also have political impact as well. The Bretton Woods agreement was the first of these but by no means the only or the last; in 1951, at the instigation of France and West Germany, the European Coal and Steel Community was established. The Community, as it became known, differed from the World Bank, its nearest counterpart in a more global sense, in one material aspect: the Community was purposely designed as a sovereign entity.

By 'sovereign' was, and is, meant that this institution derived its powers, finances, as well as its personality from its member states. By nature of its legal personality, it also holds a seat in the United Nations, sitting alongside, inter alia, its six original members. By charter, the Community, or ECSC, was dedicated to the rationalisation of the coal and steel industries of its member states, the six original members of what would become the European Economic Community, or 'common market'. In order to meet its objectives, it was also vested with a taxing power, in the form of a levy on production, which became the first international (non-imperial) tax of the twentieth century in the West.

Although the ECSC still exists today, its preeminence as

Europe's most important transborder institution has been
taken by its successor, the European Economic Community
(EEC), founded in 1957. The major purpose of the EEC was
and is to remove all tariff barriers among its members in order
to achieve a full European economic integration. In order to
facilitate the eventual dropping of tariffs, it has already
achieved a free movement of labour across members' borders, a
common agricultural policy, and has promoted free currency
movement. But as a financial institution, the EEC, as well as its
predecessor, has established one other important function: it
has acted as international borrower in its own right, fully
backed by the resources of the individual members of the EEC
themselves.

Before discussing this international borrowing and on-lend-
ing phenomenon, it should be noted that the EEC has also
instituted its own development/investment bank, the European Investment Bank (EIB). This institution has also developed its own personality in the international marketplace
although its name is something of misnomer. Rather than being
an investment bank in the traditional sense described in
Chapter 3, it is more of a development bank in that it borrows
in order to lend funds to lesser developed areas of the EEC and
to the Third World as well. In this sense, it performs the same
general functions as the World Bank, described below, also on
a global scale although its primary emphasis is regional. But
like all supranational-type organisations, its access to the
financial markets and its intermediary functions have given it a
unique niche in international finance.

This international agency function arises because the actual
borrowers of funds (EEC or EIB) are not the end-users but only
intermediaries in the process of bringing together borrower and
lender. In all cases, the agency that borrows is either itself
sovereign or backed by sovereign states. Within Europe alone,
the EEC itself borrows as well as its constituent institutions –
the ECSC, EIB and the European Atomic Energy Community
(EURATOM). Additionally, the Council of Europe is also a
frequent borrower and lender as well as the railway consortium,
Eurofima.[2]

In each case, a constituent of the agency involved approaches
it with a request for funds. If approved, the agency will provide
the money either from its own internal resources or most likely

with funds borrowed from the international capital markets. If the latter path is chosen, the agency borrowing phenomenon comes into effect.

Practically, the particular agency is approached because the constituent itself does not normally have access to the marketplace, or if it does, does not have a credit rating high enough to make funds readily available at a reasonable cost. The agency then uses its own borrowing personality to obtain the funds in its own name, normally through the bond markets in a hard currency,[3] and disburses them at the same cost to the constituent, plus a small administrative fee.

Using its own unique personality, the international agency is able to accomplish two distinct objectives. First, it is able to borrow on fine terms (normally AAA quality) because of its sovereign backing. Second, it is able to pass along this relatively cheap source of funds to borrowers often having much lower credit ratings. Thus a development bank function has been accomplished. In order to protect itself from the end borrower defaulting, the agency can ask for guarantees on the loans from third parties, usually provided by the end borrowers' commercial banks.

The international agencies currently utilising the marketplace are the European Community member institutions, as mentioned above, the other two European members, along with the World Bank, the Inter-American Development Bank, the African Development Bank, and the Asian Development Bank. As a group they form a sizeable borrowing and lending force and at any time, depending upon requirements, may have an aggregate $40–$50 billion worth of debt oustanding, denominated in most of the major currencies and occasionally in some minor currencies as well.

One important fact concerning the agencies concerns their backing. Because of it, their debt becomes an off-balance sheet (contingent) liability of the various countries providing the guarantees. Normally, this guaranty is weighted upon the individual country's participation in the agency itself. If, for instance, West Germany's share of the EEC budget is the largest, based upon GNP, then its share of the community-backed borrowings will also be the largest.

The agency function performed by the development banks is similar to the function performed in the United States by government agencies that provide liquidity for different types of loans, ranging from mortgage and student loans to export credit guarantees. As will be seen in Chapter 6, the domestic agency performs the same function as its international brethren; only the actual constituency differs.

In some cases, development banks disperse soft loans: those made to extremely needy borrowers at less than market rates. The World Bank is one example of this type of subsidising agent. Through an affiliate, the International Development Agency (IDA), loans are made at less than prevailing market rates, the difference in rates being charged to retained earnings. The borrower, normally one of the poorest nations, receives money with a long pay-back period and an intial grace period that may be ten years. This allows the end borrower to amortise the principal repayment over a long period, effectively reducing the cash outflow that it would otherwise have to pay to a more commercially-minded borrower.

Regardless of the exact nature of the development bank or its funding operation, it is still organised as a business entity in that it must make enough of a profit, either by passing along administrative costs of borrowing or by trading its own fixed income portfolio, so that it does not finish in the red. Investors in their bond issues do not need to know who the ultimate borrower is because of the levels of guaranty already in place.

The BIS was instrumental in helping to encourage development banking on an international scale. After the European institutions in particular organised in the early and late 1950s their first task was to find sources of funds in order to fulfill their objectives. The ECSC was the first institution to raise money and the first to encounter the penetration problems faced by many new borrowers in the international markets – those attached to being a new institution yet unproven as a borrower of sizeable amounts of money. In order to pave the way for ECSC, the BIS acted as paying agent for its first borrowings to ensure that the borrowed funds were channeled and disbursed properly. The role of the BIS, although somewhat short-lived in this case, helped what was to become a major international borrower of funds initially break into the marketplace by acting as a recognisable liaison.

Because of the way most of the international agencies structure their loans to their end borrowers, there have been very few actual defaults by the constituents which would in turn jeopardise repayments to the bond markets. This clean record has enabled agencies to remain prime credits in the international markets, especially during the period of financial crisis when the commercial banks with large foreign loan portfolios were not so fortunate.

Both the IMF and the World Bank have taken on additional responsibilities in the wake of the Third World debt crisis of recent years. Traditionally, the IMF made short-term loans to its member states in need, based upon economic pre-conditions, the most notable generally being the imposition of stringent economic cutbacks in the domestic economy in question in order to achieve lower domestic inflation and renewed growth. But in response to political dissatisfaction with these types of measures, calls have been made for a redefinition of the Fund's role in helping to abate the debt repayment crisis, with the hope that the new definition will entail less stringent economic measures in the member states and consequently less domestic social and political turmoil.

The World Bank has been traditionally a lender of long-term funds to needy countries and while it will remain as such it has been asked to take on additional duties, such as administering a pool of money to guaranty Third World indebtedness to the commercial banks. In both cases, these two Bretton Woods institutions have been requested to step in to fill a void in the international system that would not have been foreseen forty years ago.

INTERNATIONAL COMMERCIAL BANKING

Although international institutions are predominant at the very top of the international system their role in everyday commercial transactions is necessarily limited. The heart of the international payments mechanism is the group of commercial banks of various nationalities that conduct business on a global level. As a lumpen category, these banks form the very core of the international system per se.

Because of the problems presented by sovereignty, de facto monetary zones, and traditional trading bloc alliances, the only true international banking function that has been constant over the years has been one of the most basic: providing facilities for customers needing to borrow funds for international remittals or provide accounts for the payment of international debts. Given the lack of an official institution providing these services, the task has fallen upon, and remained with, the commercial banks. Other levels of everyday business – export-import finance, international loans, and foreign exchange dealing – are also the preserves of the commercial banks.

The nature and general functions of commercial banking are dealt with in the next chapter. However, some of their international activities are so crucial that they must be mentioned here. Although the international system is fragmented, it is the commercial banking group that gives it a cohesive element.

The major contribution of commercial banks in this context is twofold: first, they provide networking facilities whereby international payments may be transmitted from one country to another, providing the system with a clearing function. Second, they are the major market-makers in foreign exchange, providing currencies either in the spot or forward markets.

In each case, the banks also shoulder a sizeable risk in monetary transactions since either by geographical spread or by time, as evident in the fast-moving foreign exchange market, their exposure to the marketplace and credit risks can be substantial. As a result, fees for international transactions are normally somewhat higher than for a similar domestic transaction.

The other areas penetrated by commercial banks include export-import financing and the development of the offshore deposit market, most often referred to as the euromarket, or eurodollar market, for deposits. In this latter case, the taking of deposits in expatriate currencies, mainly US dollars, was in effect the recycling of the large amount of OPEC surpluses in the late 1970s to those nations or enterprises in deficit. While it may be argued that the taking of deposits, internationally or domestically, and the subsequent lending at a higher rate is part and parcel of a commercial bank's function, the explosion in deposits and loans that occurred in the 1970s was a phenomenon that cannot be simply written off as just another international banking function. The eurodollar explosion in deposits and loans helps to underscore the importance of international banking regardless of the stance one takes regarding the validity of banks recycling funds in such a manner. The fact that such massive lending was able to be accomplished on such a scale proves how quick and innovative the commercial banks were in responding to new developments in the marketplace. Export-import financing is a function that commercial banks perform in a variety of ways; some traditional and others more exotic. Perhaps the most important of them is the guaranty of an international payment on the behalf of an importer by a bank in the form of a letter of credit (lc) by which the bank guarantees to an exporter, or seller, payment for its goods or services on behalf of the importer, or buyer. In some cases, these lcs can become fully-fledged money market instruments if the draft accompanying them is presented to the guarantor bank for immediate payment. If this should be the case, a discount bill is issued which can also be sold in the money market at a rate less than face value with the holder receiving full face value at maturity. The American version of this type of bill, the bankers' acceptance, is a major instrument in the US money market. Once a commercial bank enters the import process by guaranteeing an importer's purchase, it assumes either an off-balance sheet liability or a direct short-term liability depending upon the nature the guaranty ultimately takes.

Banks have also been instrumental in developing other forms of market-related financing for imports such as forfaiting. This sort of financing is practised mainly by Swiss and German banks and involves the issuance of a series of short-term notes on the behalf of a borrower, normally in the developing world, and guaranteed by the forfaiter. The purchaser of one of these instruments receives a money market rate of interest on the notes without recourse (*á forfait*) to the ultimate borrower in the event of a default.

In these two above mentioned examples, banks can be seen to be playing a visible role in export-import financing that helps to underscore their importance in the international payments system. In most transactions involving export agencies and clients from other countries, banks often act as intermediary agents. For instance, if a company from one country approached the export credit agency of another in order to receive financing in the form of a loan so that it could purchase from one of its national companies, the agency itself would most likely use the commercial banking system as a conduit of funds in order to carry out the transaction.

While commercial banks are central to the functioning of the system, their respective central banks are also present in varying degrees and round out the spectrum of participants that effect international financial transactions, acting both in their official capacities and as investors in their own right.

CENTRAL BANKS

Central banks are rightly regarded as domestic institutions chiefly responsible for controlling the banking and monetary systems of their respective countries. But as the number of international transactions has grown geometrically and the influence of the euromarkets have made themselves felt more and more each year, the role of major central banks has become increasingly global. Now that the major money and capital markets have become linked internationally, it is no longer possible to discuss the roles of central banks in purely domestic terms.

A central bank governs its domestic banking system through monetary policy. As part of that policy, it is also responsible for the amount of money in circulation in the economy and ultimately determines whether its currency will be allowed to trade freely on the foreign exchange markets or be subject to controls. In this latter case, if exchange controls are adopted, the central bank recognises that the economy is susceptible to outside pressures and therefore controls, or seeks to control, the amount of domestic currency as well as foreign exchange that may be allowed to pass through the banking system.

In order to achieve this, the central bank can order local banks to report and sometimes limit foreign exchange transactions. If the economy of the country is highly developed it may also place restrictions on the amount of financing that a foreign company can accomplish in its domestic markets by raising local currency in the capital markets.

Following these possibilities, the role of the central banks in the international system is most closely felt in the foreign exchange markets. As indicated earlier, many do their foreign exchange dealings with the BIS although they may also trade with the commercial banks as well. Central banks trade foreign exchange for two basic reasons. First, as already mentioned, about 80 per cent of all central bank foreign exchange reserves are estimated to be held in US dollars. Thus, the banks are constantly buying and selling dollars with other currencies, including their own, in order to maintain a proper portfolio mix.

A common ratio employed in this regard is 'import cover': the number of times its foreign exchange reserves cover one month's import bill. If most of the country's trade is conducted in dollars or ultimately converted into dollars, then the central bank will trade in the market to ensure that the ratio and the covering currency are properly maintained.

Second, many central banks intervene in the foreign exchange market in order to shore up their own currencies against others individually or against a centrally quoted rate like the European Currency Unit (ECU) of the European Monetary System.[4] If a currency is perceived as too strong or weak a central bank may sell it or purchase it against others in order to stabilise its value. Local protection, or intervention, under floating exchange rates has had various connotations over the last fifteen years, including such terms as 'dirty float', indicating that a currency is not really floating in an unmanipulated manner. More recently, intervention in the foreign exchange market has become more commonplace, especially during the period of abnormally high US dollar values during the first half of the 1980s. A twofold approach now exists to market intervention that is generally recognised by those involved in international payments because of the sizeable impact either can have on the balance sheets of international corporations as well as on central banks themselves. An official intervention exists in that a central bank may redefine the value of its currency by an official devaluation or revaluation. This is only possible, however, when the currency is being quoted at some official parity or pegged central rate such as the ECU. Such actions will also affect the value of the currency against others not included in the basket or parity value calculation.

The second type of intervention has become known as 'sterilised' intervention. This name has been adopted to show that the central bank in question is intervening only to prop up or depreciate its currency against others momentarily but that the action itself should only be taken as temporary. Normally, this sort of desired effect is had by lowering or raising interest rates in the domestic economy in order to affect the exchange rate.[5] The action is not intended to alter the economic outlook for the domestic economy and is not to be taken as a long-term indication of monetary policy. In other words, the central bank is willing to sell off some of its reserves or tinker with domestic interest rates temporarily in order to achieve short-term effects rather than let the foreign exchange markets take an independent view that may eventually force it to alter policy after the fact.

Although the international system sometimes appears more as a headless body groping in the financial dark than an organised group of financial institutions, it does nevertheless function in an orderly fashion and has been able to weather many international crises. Despite the absence of an official lender of last resort, international institutions, commercial banks, and all of the other sundry financial institutions operating within it have worked together to make it function smoothly over time in order to make international financial transactions as commonplace today as domestic transactions.

NOTES

1. Toward the end of the 1970s, the SDR became used in some commercial transactions but in a very limited way. Some eurobond issues were denominated in them as well as some bank time deposits. In either case, the financial asset was a purely commercial creation; it had nothing to do with IMF policy. Any commercial bank or investment bank willing to deal in SDRs simply created an asset based upon the basket value of the currency and quoted the official IMF rate. A customer paid for the asset in his native currency and received the same, or other, currency back upon liquidation of the SDR asset.

2. Both of these supranational bodies are independent of the EEC and are organised for specific purposes. The Council of Europe is devoted to, *inter alia*, the resettlement and training of displaced workers, while Eurofima is a multinational railway consortium that purchases railway rolling stock for the national railway systems of its member states.

3. A hard currency, by definition, is one that is free to trade in the foreign exchange market; free of government regulation or other impediments such as exchange controls.

4. The European Monetary System is a financial agreement of the members of the EEC to create a basket currency, the European Currency Unit, or

ECU. The ECU is a weighted currency made of the currencies of the member states that does not include the US dollar in its central value, only the currencies of the members. In order to maintain the value of the basket, member central banks are obliged to maintain their currencies value within an agreed band.

5. 'Sterilisation' intervention technically means that a central bank practising it must make a compensating gesture on its own balance sheet when intervening in the foreign exchange market so that the market intervention does not have an inflationary effect upon the domestic economy.

2 Commercial Banking

The term 'commercial banking' originated in the nineteenth century when larger banking institutions dealt primarily with those engaged in commerce rather than the individual saver. Since then, the commercial bank has expanded its services and client base so that today it may be more appropriately called a full service banking institution. But regardless of how expansive they may have become, commercial banks still fulfil certain basic financial functions which no other single financial institution can emulate.

In financial circles, the term bank can be overused somewhat but the contemporary definition would hold that while there is a distinct difference between commercial, investment, merchant, and development banking it is the commercial bank that is most apt to perform its unique functions plus those of the other institutions, either occasionally or as part of an integrated structure on a regular basis. It is more likely to find a commercial bank underwriting securities, as an investment bank, than it is to find an investment bank offering deposit accounts. As the traditional lines of banking demarcation begin to crumble in both the United States and Britain, it is the commercial bank which will probably benefit most because of its sheer size, range of contacts, and its branching system.

The basic difference between a commercial bank and its nearest competitors lies both in function and in the range within which that function is performed. Essentially, a commercial bank offers transaction and deposit accounts through which its customers may pay for and receive funds that are the heart of their respective businesses, or spending and savings functions. Equally, the commercial bank is able to redeploy the savings of its depositors as loans to various entities in need of funds, whether the need come from an individual or from a business. In this latter instance, it is the ability to make commercial loans that separates commercial banks from other sorts of depository/lending institutions. The combination of function and range separates this sort of institution from its competition by redeploying deposits in the widest range of loans possible.

The most popular form of transaction account is the *demand deposit* or checking account, also known as a *current account* in Britain. As with all deposit accounts held by a bank, regardless of terms or interest paid, deposit accounts are booked as liabilities by banks on their balance sheets. Loans, on the other hand, are booked as assets since they earn a rate of interest paid by the borrower. The larger the commercial bank, the more diffuse its asset/liability base will be. Deposits from savers may find their way into a loan made to an individual, multinational business, or foreign government in a developing country.

In Britain, the largest of the commercial banks are generally referred to as *clearing banks*, or simply 'clearers'. The functional connotation of the name is due to the fact that the clearing system for banks in the United Kingdom is owned by the six largest commercial banks. The Bankers Clearing House thus gives its owners their name, clearers.[1] This group of six does not include the Scottish banks.

In both countries, the traditional deposit sources of funds offered by commercial banks has begun to expand in recent years. Traditionally, banks offered only checking (current) accounts and time deposits to customers. The checking or current account offered no interest return because of its frequent transaction nature plus the fact that interest could be relatively hard to calculate on a amount constantly changing, especially before the advent of computers and advanced telecommunications.

But with the arrival of computerised banking and competition for funds from other financial intermediaries, demand deposits began to pay interest although it is usually less than that paid on traditional time deposits that do not fill the transaction function and therefore are less volatile by balance as a result. Today, interest-bearing checking accounts are in use in both the United States and Britain, with the United States having the clear lead in both types offered and volume per capita invested as of this writing.

Deposits are a commercial bank's major source of funds. Over the years, other institutions and financal products have provided competition for this once natural, almost captive, inflow. But before looking at some of the more contemporary problems of commercial banks, their major functions will be examined.

GENERAL FUNCTIONS

On the broadest level, the functions of commercial banks will vary depending upon the nature of the economy in which they operate. In some small economies, commercial banks perform functions normally associated with governmental agencies in larger, industrialised countries, such as the issuance of currency. But for the most part, the role of commercial banks tends to follow general lines although the means by which they accomplish them can be done through different sorts of products, or financial packaging.

A bank's chief role is to take in deposits from its retail or commercial customers and make these funds available for lending. This is known as the process of credit creation whereby the funds of net savers are channeled to borrowers in need of money. Through this process, the bank becomes a debtor to those loaning it money and its borrowers in turn become debtors of the bank.

The difference between the rate of interest a bank pays its depositors and the rate at which it lends to borrowers is known as its 'spread' and represents its gross margin of profit. It is this fundamental function that makes a bank a financial intermediary, reallocating funds from those in surplus to those in need.

The process of credit creation is not left entirely to banks' discretion, however. While the commercial decision concerning who may borrow and at what particular rate is solely within the bank's providence, the overall process is controlled by the monetary authorities, namely the central bank, of the country involved. This will be discussed in another section below because the amount of credit available in an economy at any point in time has a profound impact upon economic activity.

The same is true of another phenomenon found in this simple deposit taking/lending process that is solely the preserve of commercial banks – namely the ability to create money as well as credit. Money creation can be accomplished by no other single financial institution; it is currently solely in the realm of commercial banking. How this occurs will also be dealt with in that later section.

In addition to making loans, banks also channel funds of depositors into the investment securities markets, thereby providing a strong institutional bulk-buying power to the financial markets. Normally, these investments are limited to government securities and municipal securities. These securities provide a rate of return normally higher than that paid to depositors and also provide banks with investment or asset liquidity, something loans cannot accomplish.

Another general function of banks is providing customers with fiduciary services, again through the securities markets. This is accomplished through trust departments or trust divisions. Individuals or companies place money to be invested with the bank and it provides the expertise and executes the investment decision for which it charges a fee. The term 'fiduciary' enters here because the money is to be invested at the discretion of the bank on behalf of the individual rather than having the investor do the actual investing himself. In this respect, the bank acts as investment advisor to the client and also holds the securities in safekeeping. This is one area in which banks compete with many other investment organisations on an active basis for the right to manage the public's money, especially that of large institutional investors such as pension funds or insurance companies.

A large portion of a commercial bank's activities has been extended overseas through branches in order to engage in overseas financing for customers, whether they be domestic clients doing business overseas or purely foreign sources of business. In many cases, this business is merely an extension of the types of services provided domestically with a foreign exchange element sometimes added.

The international aspect of commercial banking has grown geometrically since the end of the Second World War and, in some cases, the international trading activities of a bank can prove to be some of its most profitable. Areas such as foreign exchange trading, both spot and forward, export-import financing, and syndicated lending have provided profitable additions to the general areas already mentioned. In some cases, banks were able to capitalise on new developments in the international marketplace and, in many cases, played the role of intermediary not between savers and borrowers but between the savers and the genuinely poor.

As mentioned earlier, the banks' margin of gross profit is its spread; before costs are subtracted. This is one of the major differences between a commercial bank and an investment bank. As traditional lines of demarcation between the two sectors continue to crumble, it becomes more and more difficult to make general statements about the differences between the two but in the matter of profit, it is still true to say that a commercial bank derives profit from the spread between liability payment and asset revenue. Investment banks, on the other hand, profit by successful security trading, fixed underwriting and other fees generally negotiated with the client.

This matter of fee provides a convenient introduction to the structure of commercial banking since it is in structure, as well as in function, that the unique nature of commercial banking is found. As it continues to change complexion due to financial innovation, only a structural discussion will help explain many functions which are now shared with other financial intermediaries.

TREASURY OPERATIONS

The actual day-to-day operations of a bank in the marketplace are assigned to the treasury department. The purpose of this division is to ensure that a bank's reserves, cash on hand, and investment portfolio are invested at the highest rate of return possible given constrictions on the maturity length of the liquid or near liquid investments held. Cash on hand is usually placed in overnight funds while other monies are placed in short-term or government-backed securities exposing the institution to interest rate risk but not usually to credit risk.

The breakdown of a bank's assets, other than loans, follows governmental regulations plus a prudent desire to maintain as liquid a position as possible in order to meet any unanticipated cash demands in point of time. If a depositor's money is not rechannelled into a loan it will find its way into the money markets or securities markets so that the bank can book an asset opposite the liability to the depositor.

But not all of a depositor's funds will be loaned or invested. This is due to *reserve requirements* stipulating that a certain percentage of each deposit taken in must be held as primary reserves. These are used to ensure that there will be funds on hand should the bank's depositors decide to withdraw funds. On the regulatory side of the coin, the amount of reserves to be held against the deposit is a tool in the arsenal of the monetary authorities that regulate bank behaviour. The actual reserve level depends upon the desire of the central bank to control the supply of money in the financial system.

Organisationally, the treasury department is made up of traders who operate within the money markets, buying and selling short-term funds and/or securities in order to maximise the yield levels required by the bank. The regulatory authorities do not require any specific yields to be maintained here; the amount that can be earned will ultimately be charged to the bank's profit or loss.

As an example, imagine a bank taking in a deposit for $1 million, at a deposit rate of 10 per cent for one year. This money is part of its source of funds and will need a corresponding asset to be booked at a rate in excess of 10 per cent if the transaction is to be profitable. If the money is not loaned, it will be invested in short-term securities or assets of some sort. After the appropriate reserve requirement is applied, say 10 per cent, $900 000 is available for investment. Because of the requirement, the investment rate will now have to be marginally higher than it would have been if the amounts were calculated on a straight one to one basis.

Of all the available choices, assume the bank settles on a deposit in the inter-bank market for $11\frac{1}{4}$ per cent. It places the money at a similar maturity to the one year it offered its depositor and takes the rate differential as its profit. In this case, the original depositor will be paid $100 000 interest (assuming no compound interest) while the bank receives $101 250 interest on its principal of $900 000.

Banks are able to offer deposits at less than the prevalent money market rate of interest because of the service they provide depositors plus security of principal. There is nothing to actually prohibit the depositor from by-passing the bank and

make a similar sort of deposit himself but if he is seeking
security of his money and does not have relatively large sums to
invest institutionally then the retail function of the bank is
probably his safest avenue. And the individual is also establish-
ing a history of dealing with a particular bank which can pave
the way for further dealings in the future, such as the extension
of a loan or other lines of credit. While the amount set aside for
reserves can be over-looked in explaining a bank's normal
investment function, it is nevertheless at the heart of the
banking system's ability to create credit. If the reserve requirement was lower than 10 per cent, the return on the inter-bank
investment would have been even greater. Conversely, if it had
been higher the inter-bank deposit might not have proved a
viable investment at all. In the same vein, the level of reserve
requirements will help to determine what types of loans the
bank will eventually make in order to balance its books while
seeking what it perceives to be an adequate return on funds
placed in the market.

Reserves are broken into two categories, primary and
secondary. Generally speaking, primary reserves are those cash
assets held by a bank to meet its official requirements. Whether
or not these assets are able to earn a rate of interest depends
upon the monetary authority setting the rules for the banking
system. For instance, reserves required by the Federal Reserve
of its member banks are held as interest-free cash deposits at
the Federal Reserve Bank for the region in which the particular
commercial bank is located. In times of high interest rates
especially, these idle reserves represent opportunity losses,
given that otherwise they might be held in Treasury bills
yielding a market rate.

When American interest rates shifted into a significantly
higher plane in the late 1970s, many banks took the ultimate
step of withdrawing from the Federal Reserve system and
submitted themselves instead to bank regulatory authorities in
their home states in order to avoid this problem of idle cash
reserves. The Federal Reserve (Fed) thus experienced a net
withdrawal of banks from its jurisdiction. The primary motive
behind this move was the interest that could be earned on some
state regulated reserves *vis-à-vis* the interest free status of
balances held at the Fed. Theoretically, even if a state had
higher reserve requirements than did the Fed, a high rate of

interest on them could offset the increased ratio and still spell more return for the banks involved.

British clearing banks did not undergo the same sort of withdrawl phenomenon despite the fact that they too must hold their reserve assets as interest free balances at the Bank of England. Due to the unitary nature of the British government system, no other banking authorities are present in the financial system other than the central bank, as can be found in the American federal system.

In addition to market operations directly tied to client business, banks also trade among themselves in the marketplace in order to manage their own portfolios and this too is a treasury function. This can be seen most clearly in the foreign exchange markets; an activity not indulged in by all banks but certainly by the larger commercial banks with international interests. Banks enter into foreign exchange contracts with customers desirous of either buying or selling foreign currencies either spot or forward. They also take positions for their own accounts in order to either take advantage of anticipated rate changes or to offset an exposure in a currency other than their own. This can occur regardless of whether the bank is taking in deposits in a foreign currency or making a loan in the currency.

The treasury function is therefore at the heart of a bank's operations because it is the way that funding and the deployment of funds is managed. It is normally thought of in terms of asset management although it also becomes a factor in funding itself. If, for instance, a bank desires to raise funds for lending it may do so by issuing negotiable certificates of deposit, or CDs, in the money market. Rather than take in money through customer deposits, it raises the funds in the form of marketable deposits and uses the proceeds to fund lending activities. This too is part of the treasury function because it is an interest rate-driven activity and requires a specialised knowledge of the money markets and how they operate.

LENDING ACTIVITIES

The lending activities of banks are what differentiates them from other financial institutions that also grant loans to customers. Although some banks limit their activities to a wholesale (institutional or corporate) base, their lending activities are generally considered universal in that they offer a full range of loan services to clients, regardless of geographical location. This can be seen most clearly in the types of loan offered by the larger commercial banks, ranging from automobile loans, consumer loans, and mortgages on one hand to commercial and industrial loans and internationally syndicated loans on the other. Some of the world's largest banks are the largest creditors of Third World developing nations while at the same time having some of the largest portfolios of auto loans as well.

Since loans are assets of banks their composition and quantity are directed by portfolio limits; the same sort of constraints that an individual would set for himself when investing in the securities markets. If a bank determines that home mortgages should comprise no more than say 15 per cent of its overall loan book it will not exceed that limit, at least temporarily, and will set its lending rates accordingly. A bank actively seeking home loans will offer more advantageous rates than those not doing so; the higher the interest rate charged the less likely the bank is to originate mortgages.

The most serious pitfall a bank can encounter occurs when a certain amount of loans become non-performing; that is, the borrower effectively defaults in its payments of principal or interest. This interrupts the projected cash flow of the lender and forces it to pay depositors' interest out of other resources, thereby cutting its profit margin. If non-performing loans increase, eventually a loan loss reserve will have to be created in order to offset unforeseen or anticipated defaults in the future.

In order to determine the credit worthiness of a potential borrower, banks perform credit analyses of borrowers to establish whether debt service can be made in timely fashion. This function is one of the bedrocks upon which banking is founded. Unfortunately, the principles of credit worthiness can be difficult to apply to the full range of a bank's international customers. Take as an example an individual applying for a mortgage loan. Financial ability to meet debt service and amortisation of principal is determined by an individual's income and actually depends very little upon his future ability to meet these current financial obligations. The reason is simple: the loan is secured by the property itself. If the individual defaults on the loan the bank can foreclose the mortgage in order to protect its asset (the loan).

If, on the other hand, a bank makes a loan to a foreign government, the ability to pay back is determined by the government's financial position (balance of payments, trade balance, budget deficit or surplus) and is usually not secured. So if a sovereign state's revenues should drop and it finds itself unable to repay its debts, there is little recourse other than the courts to retrieve the funds. Recent experience has shown that when the total amount of debt outstanding is quite sizeable, banks prefer to reschedule these loans rather than declare them in default in the hope that downstream revenues of the borrower will again increase. Ironically, this is a more modern version of Mark Twain's nineteenth-century adage: if you owe a bank a dollar and cannot pay you have a problem. If you owe it a million dollars and cannot pay, it has a problem.

Loans are segmented into different types so that they are a reflection of economic activity on the part of the borrowing units. The category of commercial and industrial loans is the most carefully monitored on a short-term basis and is reported weekly in the United States along with other monetary statistics such as the growth of the money supply. These loans are a good indicator of the amount of inventory financing conducted by business. Since they are normally made on a short-term basis they also provide a leading indication of how businesses view, and are coping with, the economy.

Within their lending activities, banks are able to perform one economic function that no other financial institution possesses; the ability to create money. In the example already used, loan making was seen as the asset deployment of a liability, namely a deposit or a CD. When the bank places depositors' funds in the loan sector, it creates credit; the multiplier being the inverse of the reserves, or $1/R$. Reserves themselves become the central focus of money creation; on the particular day that banks report their reserve levels to their respective central banks, some will be holding excess reserves while others will be short. Those banks that lend excess reserves to others in fact create money by doing so. A loan to a customer, even when matched by a deposit, does not technically have any effect in the marketplace until the reserve level has been met.

Because banks have this particular power their activities in extending credit become of vital importance to the state of the economy as a whole. And there is another aspect of bank lending, international lending, that has burgeoned within the last decade while at the same time eluding monetary authorities in many cases.

During the 1970s, the international banking community grew in geometrical proportions because of the impact of oil price increases. Dollar balances rose in European banks, mainly in London, Paris, and Switzerland as OPEC countries deposited much of their new found wealth in the euromarkets. As eurobanks took in these large deposits, mainly in US dollars, their ability to make dollar denominated loans increased dramatically and many countries took advantage of this surplus to borrow for domestic purposes.

As eurolending increased, it became apparent that the traditional credit multiplier had taken on a new dimension because these eurobanks were not subject to American reserve requirements. For example, the London branch of a Swiss bank was able to lend out 100 per cent of a deposit while its domestic American counterpart could lend out only that portion not covered by reserve requirements. So the eurobanks had a special advantage in lending, regardless of their nationality; by lending out a deposit on a one-to-one ratio they were able to earn a higher rate of return on their newly created assets than a domestic counterpart.

Eurobanks were able to avoid reserve requirements because they act as external banks in their host country if they deal in currencies other than that of the host. Sometimes this international lending was done from finance subsidiaries of banks in Europe rather than from the parent or branches directly. But regardless of origin, the eurobanking system became the favourite source of funds for many international borrowers.

Loans in general are usually made by a sole bank to its customer unless the amount involved is quite large and would prove burdensome or violate a bank's individual limits to a single borrower. When this occurs, the large amount may be syndicated, or underwritten, among a number of banks, limiting the amount of exposure incurred by any one institution. This process is referred to as syndicated lending and is the method employed to provide funds to unusually large borrowers, who either take it in one large lump sum or keep it in ready reserve as a draw-down facility.

This was how most of the large amounts of international borrowed funds were packaged during the borrowing explosion in the wake of oil price rises. The original bank that initiated the deal and other terms of the loan would provide the pricing mechanism and then offer participations to other banks in the international community.[2] Through syndication, a large loan, say \$500 million, could be sold to as many as fifty to one hundred banks, each taking a fractional amount.

Borrowing funds against which there were no reserve requirements has provoked much controversy concerning the traditional functions of banks and has raised the inevitable question of how much money and/or credit was being created in the process. In one sense, the answer became less inportant than the practical effects of such loans after the Third World debt crisis began in the early 1980s. As more and more countries began rescheduling their syndicated debts, the lending process itself fell off sharply. As a result, many borrowers have turned to the traditional bond markets as a source of funds. As long as syndicated lending does not blossom again the economic questions raised about its characteristics will remain secondary to the economic consequences it has created.

On the asset side of a bank's balance sheet, it becomes obvious that loans are as volatile in their own right as are investments in the securities markets. While the latter exposes a bank to interest rate risk only (because most of these securities are issued by the government or are government-backed) the former exposes it to a credit risk as well that is significantly more difficult to gauge.

TRUST ACTIVITIES

As financial intermediaries, banks also perform trust activities on behalf of their clients. This type of operation is usually separated from their commercial banking activities per se through an officially organised trust department that manages funds on a fiduciary basis, through power of attorney. Trust activities alone would make many commercial banks some of the largest financial managers in their respective economies, leaving their normal operations aside.

Banks manage portfolios of securities, including common stock, for a wide range of both retail and institutional clients. This function includes the actual investment decision, its execution, securities safekeeping, and disbursal of funds. It is important to remember that these functions are provided for active clients as well as estates since many times banks will take over the estate for someone deceased and manage it for the heirs.

Although banks may purchase securities for clients, in the United States they are prohibited from either owning or underwriting the same sorts of corporate securities. According to the provisions of the Glass-Steagall Act of 1933, banks may not underwrite corporate securities (stocks or bonds) in order to ensure that the underwriting decision is separated from the fiduciary investment decision. Following this, American banks do not hold corporate securities for their own accounts nor do they trade them. But they are free to invest in them on a prudent basis for others.

Trust departments also may provide certain types of security related operations for clients. They may provide paying agent facilities for dividend or interest payments on behalf of a company, oversee assets pledged to bond holders through a bond's indenture, and manage a company's sinking funds (monies used to retire some bonds prior to maturity). In recent years, a good deal of bank business has come from the administration of interest rate swaps on behalf of companies that have outstanding bonds.

These sorts of activities, while general to commercial banks, will vary from country to country depending upon the combination of securities and banking laws. While strict delineation of these activities is found in the United States, Canada, Japan, and Britain, some of the continental European countries take a less strict position of a bank's operations in the securities markets and investment matters. It should not necessarily be assumed that investor protection suffers as a result; in most cases the regulations are based traditionally upon the role of equity markets in the country's economy.

Those countries with the strictest regulations are those with the most active equity markets. Others tend to favour bonds as the primary source of company financing. As a result, equity investment is not popular and bond financing and investment supersedes it, with a different element of risk attached. Therefore, the trust departments of many continental banks invest many more bonds in their clients' portfolios than equities, with substantially less risk. In many cases, local regulations recognise this trend and do not separate it from commercial banking.

BANKS AND MONETARY POLICY

Because of their central role as intermediaries in an economy, banks are at the centre of monetary policy as set down by the appropriate monetary authorities. This special role as the focus of governmental economic policy falls upon banks because of their special ability to create money as well as credit.

In order to understand the impact of policy upon commercial banks, it is useful to consider a financial system as a whole, although this cannot be done in the United States without some prior legal qualifications. It is much easier to contemplate in Britain because of the unitary nature of the banking system. American banks differ from each other by the nature of their charter; they may be either federally or state chartered. In the former case, if a bank obtains its charter from the federal government (specifically from the Comptroller of the Currency) then it automatically falls under the aegis of the superintendent of the federal banking system, the Federal Reserve. Operating through a board of governors and twelve reserve districts, the Fed is an independent body that oversees monetary policy. Because of its organisation and independence from any other governmental jurisdiction, the Fed single-handedly plays the central role in determining the availability of credit and interest rates but has no hand in directly determining fiscal policy. So unlike some countries where economic policies are centralised, the Fed actually operates independently, both operationally and ideologically, from the fiscal policy-making side of government.

Until recently, the Fed controlled only those banks having a federal charter. However, according to the provisions of the Depository Institutions Deregulation and Monetary Control Act of 1980, all banks and depository institutions in the United

States became subject to the Fed's reserve requirements. But the distinction between federally chartered and state chartered remains although the differentials that existed between Fed reserve requirements and state reserve requirements have gone by the board.

In reality, most of the large American banks having recognisable names doing international business are in fact federally chartered, especially the 'money centre' banks located in the major financial centres, issuing short-term debt obligations in their own names. These are the banks that, by virtue of their size, trade most of the nation's money market paper and have the largest amount of deposits. Banks that are not a part of the system are, as a group, smaller in size and tend to operate regionally or locally but still follow the larger banks in the marketplace when determining interest rate levels on accounts and types of products offered to the public.

This dualism, obviously greater before 1980, does not exist in Britain. All commercial banking institutions, as well as all depository institutions, fall under the aegis of the Bank of England whose broad powers have evolved over time. From the broadest perspective, both central banks perform many similar functions; only the legislative background tends to differ.

Membership in the Fed also spells an element of depositor protection although it is in a limited form. Federally chartered banks *ipso facto* become members of the Federal Deposit Insurance Corporation (FDIC) which insures small deposits up to a maximum of $100 000. Many state chartered banks voluntarily belong to the corporation as well, although they are not obligated to do so. However, this body does not insure large deposits of more than $100 000.

Depositor protection of this nature does not exist in Britain where individual bank problems, when they occur, tend to be ironed out by both the Bank of England and the major clearing banks. This more unofficial method of protection is obviously a less formal arrangement than the American model and the depositor cannot be guaranteed that he or she will receive 100 pence on the pound in return if a bank should fail.

Central banks influence the activities of commercial banks in several ways; notably through the reserve requirement imposed on member banks, open market operations in the money market, controlling the discount rate,[3] and what American commentators have come to call 'jawboning', or 'moral suasion'. The last technique involves communicating to banks a desired effect rather than a specific policy statement. The first two require the most explanation since they are essentially the most difficult.

Reserve requirements and their effects on the banking and financial system have already been noted above. For every unit of currency a bank takes in on deposit, a specific percentage must be held back in reserve. So the bank is not effectively able to lend out the same amount. The net cumulative effect is to ensure that cash is on hand to satisfy any potential demand for funds. As mentioned earlier, if the requirement is set at 10 per cent, $90 of a $100 deposit is free to be placed on loan.

If the central bank decides to clamp down on credit creation, it could raise the requirement to say 15 per cent, reducing the multiplier from 10 to 6.67 (1/10 as opposed to 1/15). The banks could previously lend $90 under the 10 per cent requirement; now they may lend out only $85.

Through this control, the availability of credit will diminish. This simple explanation does not explain the interest rate implications of the rise in requirements, however. If reserve requirements are increased, interest rates will rise with them. The interest rate implication of such a move is found in the amount of funds now available for lending. Since the banks are now constrained by an additional $5 on lending, they will have to charge more for the loan on the $85 than they did on the $90. This will raise borrowing costs and possibly make it prohibitive for some borrowers to apply for loans.

Ultimately, not only the cost of borrowing from banks will rise but so too will borrowing in the money markets. Larger corporate clients may decide to issue their own form of short-term debt rather than tap their bank, and those borrowing costs will also rise as more and more companies take this avenue of approach. And as money market rates rise, so too will the return demanded by depositors and investors in short-term deposits or securities.

This rather simple explanation fails to take into account the fact that monetary policy usually unfolds in a concerted way rather than through one technique alone. While manipulation of the reserve requirement is perhaps the best known of the techniques used by central banks it is often used in conjunction with open market operations which have a more immediate effect upon interest rate levels and concomitantly upon the amount of funds available for lending.

Open market operations were originally associated most often with the Fed but after the international monetary turbulence of the late 1970s and early 1980s other major central banks began to adopt them as well; at least by disclosing that they were actually performing them officially. Basically, open market operations are the same in most countries although the American example has been discussed here because it is the most commonly employed variety.

As employed by the Fed, the term 'open market' operations means that the central bank purchases or sells short-term Treasury securities in the money market for its own account. If the central bank wants to siphon funds out of the banking system, it sells securities thereby removing cash from dealers' hands. Conversely, if it wants to inject funds into the system, it will purchase securities, paying cash and thereby adding funds into the system.

While it is generally correct to say that funds are either made available or siphoned from the system, more specifically it is the investment banking and commercial banking community that is the focus of Fed behaviour, not the general public. The investment banking community enters the picture here because many investment banks are primary dealers of Treasury securities. But while they are the dealing focus, the cash involved in the trading is really what the central bank focuses upon. Although there are over thirty investment and commercial banks designated as primary securities dealers, it is where they keep their transaction accounts that really matters in this process because that is where the supply of money will be controlled.

The dealers' bank accounts are the ultimate focus of the Fed's actions. Depending upon the sort of operation performed, the bank account will either be debited or credited accordingly, thereby affecting the supply of money available. Concomitantly, reserve requirements also come into consideration when affecting the amount of loanable funds at the disposal of the commercial bank providing the account facilities.

Outright buying and selling of Treasury bills is also combined with two-sided transactions equally designed to either add or drain funds on a temporary basis. In some instances, the Fed may enter into a sale/purchase agreement whereby it sells bills into the dealing community and at the same time agrees to buy them back at a later date at a specific price. This is technically known as a repurchase agreement, or repo, since both the Fed and its customer know the terms of the initial and subsequent transactions.

The opposite of a repo is a reverse repurchase agreement, or reverse repo, sometimes also called 'matched sales'. In this case, the first transaction is a purchase and the subsequent transaction a sale, except when the initiator of the transaction is the lender of funds. Repos and reverses are practised both by the Fed and by the dealer community so the terminology and techniques are the same but the net overall effects are quite different. The Fed can practice either method as they are defined; a dealer is usually only a borrower initiating a transaction and another dealer lending him funds is only a party to a repo, not the originator of a reverse.

As a lender of funds, the Fed's actions in the repo market are closely watched so that other money market dealers and participants can gauge the scope of its activities. For instance, if the Fed is doing repos, it is usually interpreted as a bullish sign; that is, as ultimate lender the Fed is providing liquidity and not signalling a tightening of reserves. If, on the other hand, the Fed is doing reverses it is borrowing funds from the system and that action is taken to be generally bearish for reserves and interest rates. So the difference between a repo and a reverse is not in the actual mechanics of the transaction, although important, but in the posture the central bank is taking in the money market.

Equally important to remember here is that the Fed trades these securities for its own account and does not perform ordinary, everyday transactions for the American Treasury. Treasury securities happen to be the tools of monetary policy but do not imply a direct link to the Treasury per se. In its market operations, the Fed acts as any other security dealer in terms of day-to-day market mechanics with the simple but yet overriding consideration that it also happens to be the central bank. But whether it is long or short securities at any given point in time involves not just another dealer's position but in many cases a fundamental stance toward monetary policy, at least in the short term.[4]

Open market operations are similar in Britain and are conducted by the Bank of England via the clearing banks. Technically, there is a slight difference in method here because the operations can also be considered to include the Bank's operations in the discount market as well; that is, the operations it performs with the discount houses thereby affecting the liquidity of commercial banks indirectly. One other difference in the methods of the two central banks is that open market operations in Britain can also be taken to include UK government bonds in addition to three-month Treasury bills and other types of short-term commercial paper as well.[5]

This peculiarly British institution known as the discount house also figures prominently in monetary policy and deserves mention here although it is not a commercial bank in the remotest sense of the word. Discount houses form the heart of the London money market and act as intermediaries providing liquidity in the secondary money market. However, they are nevertheless classified as recognised banks by the 1979 Banking Act.

The function of the discount houses is to provide liquidity to the UK banking system by discounting short-term obligations, usually Treasury bills, for those institutions in need of funds. They stand between their client and the Bank of England so they become the focal point of monetary policy. An institution in need of funds sells bills to the discount house, which takes a small spread for the function it performs. In such a manner, they supply funds to banks in need by selling the bills to those with surplus cash. The Bank of England in turn will re-discount bills for the discount houses. So the central bank maintains a direct link with the money market and the rates of interest prevalent at any given point in time.

Another official tactic that can be adopted by a central bank is to raise or lower its discount rate, the rate by which it lends reserves to its banking system. In the United States, the discount rate, as set by the Fed, is fixed until officially changed again; it is a rate set by fiat although it obviously follows other money market rates. Generally it is considered to be a lagging indicator of money market conditions, at least in the United States. Reading the signals given off by the changes in the discount rate are not simple since they tend to be based upon historical information already taken account of in the market place. A lowering of the discount rate would suggest that the Fed is happy to see rates fall even further. An unchanged stance following the same sort of money market conditions would suggest that the rate is as low as the Fed would like to see it go for the time being.

A direct parallel to the American discount rate is not found in Britain. The closest type of rate would be that on call money; the rate charged on funds by banks to the discount houses. When the banks find themselves short they may call the money in, so effectively the rate at which reserves trade, and are called, is ultimately controlled by the Bank of England. This call money is more similar to federal funds trading in the United States than it is to the discount rate.[6]

The fourth general tool of monetary policy is known as 'jawboning' or moral suasion. This is an unofficial method whereby a central bank makes its feelings known to commercial banks without resorting to official monetary policy. Instead it relies upon consultations and strong indications of its own desires without invoking the official tools at its disposal.

TYPES OF COMMERCIAL BANKING ORGANISATION

Commercial banks vary greatly in their organisational natures, despite the fact that they all perform essentially the same operations. The structure varies from country to country; in Britain and the United States commercial banks are very similar despite the differences in the legal and political environments in which they operate. The Anglo-American model of a commercial bank varies greatly, however, from the continental European institution providing both commercial and investment banking under one roof.

American commercial banks are enveloped in a bevy of laws restricting their functions both legally and geographically. Although many of these measures are still in force at the time of this writing, they may well indeed be rescinded in the future because of the quickly changing financial environment. In the interim, these restrictions are being quickly circumvented by both necessity and financial innovation.

British banks are essentially free of these sorts of restrictions although there are differences in the English and Scottish banking systems which will be noted below. As will be seen, the British commercial bank grew in similar fashion to the American historically because investment banking functions have traditionally been practised by the merchant banks. The most comprehensive banking institution is the German/Swiss model incorporating commercial and investment banking services under one roof. No effective prohibitions exist separating these functions and the operational classification of these institutions is referred to as a 'universal' bank. Because of the close proximity of these operations, these institutions tend to dominate the financial services sectors of their respective economies.

The American model, on the other hand, appears fragmented, divided by legislation dating from the earlier part of the century. American banks are still not permitted to branch across state lines; they were originally prohibited from doing so by the McFadden Act of 1927. Therefore, branch banking is confined to the home state of the parent. This does not prohibit banks from opening branches abroad, however. But the geographical limitations imposed by the McFadden Act are beginning to crumble. Banking operations have indeed begun to expand across state lines through the use of the bank holding company, used to buy other depository institutions in sound financial health or institutions that would otherwise fail. In the former case, the United States Supreme Court has allowed regional banking mergers crossing state lines in order to centralise the balkanised banking networks in some areas. In the latter instance, some institutions have bought up those in another state that otherwise would have failed; the accepted premise being that a solvent bank with out of state ownership is better than an indigenous insolvent one.

Banks have crossed traditional lines in other financial services areas such as credit card operations and specialised areas such as mortgage lending without incurring the wrath of regulatory authorities. Again, the organisational way by which they were able to do so was through the existence of the holding company; an organisational form that became popular in the 1960s. Holding companies are in effect the parent corporation of both the bank and the other specialised financial subsidiaries that own the capital stock of both categories. So when a bank appears to be crossing acceptable borders through a subsidiary it is actually being migratory through the holding company, not the bank itself. Since all large banks are now organised in this fashion, the McFadden Act has not been violated, only circumvented.

Commercial banks have been prohibited from engaging in investment banking activities by the Glass-Stegall Act of 1934. This separation of function has prevented American banks from being truly universal in the continental sense; that is, offering a full range of traditional banking services. Being widespread geographically is not the connotation of 'universal'. According to the provisions of the Act, banks may not underwrite or trade in corporate securities, whether they be stocks or bonds. This legislation was passed after the 1929 crash in order to prevent banks from underwriting securities, trading them, and investing in them at the same time. It should be noted that this legislation does not prohibit banks from underwriting or trading US Government securities or those of municipalities or government agencies. Banks will underwrite municipal securities both for tax reasons as well as for goodwill reasons, especially if the municipality is the state or within the state in which they reside.

In recent years, commercial banks have begun to expand into investment or merchant banking operations nevertheless. Large money centre banks have been underwriting commercial paper obligations of corporate borrowers technically because these short-term notes mature in less than 270 days and are not classified as a security as such by the Securities and Exchange Commission (SEC). They have also become involved in private placements for corporate borrowers for essentially the same reason; since this type of bond borrowing is not listed with the SEC, banks are free to arrange their terms and placement. Equally, banks have underwritten the more traditional type of bond for corporate clients but in order to do so they have had to expand as investment banks in the euromarket.

Commercial banks' paths to the euromarkets have been accomplished around and through existing legislation that would otherwise prohibit them from practising investment banking at home. Because of the increased demands of international business, even in the earlier part of the century, banks were permitted to open specialised subsidiaries to engage in international finance in other states before the advent of the holding company. The one stipulation concerning these subsidiary operations was that they must engage in international business, not domestic.

The original legislation that made this expansion possible was the Edge Act of 1919. Banks were allowed to open subsidiaries in other states as long as they engaged in international activities only. Basically, the Edge Act expanded upon an older agreement previously negotiated (1916) that allowed banks to branch into foreign countries provided that the Federal Reserve was in agreement. Hence the origin of the name still in use today; Edge Act and Agreement Corporations, an umbrella term meaning specialised domestic subsidiaries domestically and branches abroad.

Edge Act and Agreement Corporations now engage in a wide variety of international banking and finance activities from their domestic bases. Although banks are permitted to establish branches abroad they were not, however, allowed to own shares of foreign banking subsidiaries. Through the Edge Act they are permitted to own equity in a foreign corporation and thus were able to establish themselves in international investment banking through overseas (mainly London) merchant banking subsidiaries, engaged in fee-generated business centred in the euromarkets.

The British banking system has evolved along similar lines for different historical reasons. Commercial and investment banking have been separated traditionally because of the independent development of these different types of financial institutions over time. While commercial banks have dominated the traditional clearing function, the accepting houses, or merchant banks, have dominated the fee generating business, but not exactly in the same manner as American investment banks have. This will be seen in the next chapter.

A major structural difference exists between the English and Scottish clearing banks. Although there is no prohibition against branch banking in the United Kingdom, historically certain banks have confined themselves to activities within a certain part of the country. Since the original formations, however, bank mergers have created a situation where what by name appears to be a distinct banking operation operating in a particular area may in fact be owned by one of the London clearers.

The Scottish banking system is dominated by three clearers at present.[7] The major difference between the Scottish and the English systems is that the Scottish clearers retain the right of note issue. Although the amount of notes they can actually create and circulate is limited, this function nevertheless makes them distinct, although in fact for every note created within their system they must effectively hold a Bank of England note in reserve.

The other feature peculiar to the Scottish system is that it uses the London clearing banks as its own depository for working cash balances and keeps little on deposit at the Bank of England. Scottish banks also have less rigid cash and liquid asset ratios imposed upon them by the central bank than do the English clearers.

DISINTERMEDIATION AND THE COMMERCIAL BANKS

The traditional commercial banking system in both the United States and Britain has undergone radical changes, beginning in the mid and late 1970s. These changes have been more pronounced in America because of the labyrinthine legal environment surrounding banks and the types of accounts and services they are, or were able, to offer. But the fact still remains that banks in both countries now have a somewhat different complexion than they used to. In one particular instance, the changes have been brought about by a combination of differences in the product lines they offer, spurred by a new regulatory environment.

This generic change has been most pronounced in the United States because of the individual saver's attempt to maximise yield on his savings. Beginning in the mid 1970s, investment firms began offering money market mutual funds based upon

short-term money market instruments. These funds are organised as mutual funds, or unit trusts, and offer investors a rate
of return near the prevalent institutional money market interest
rates. When the investor buys a share of the fund, he effectively
buys shares which pay him the prevalent rate minus a commission of some sort.

Money market mutual funds were originally offered at a time
when American banks were still constrained in the amount of
interest they could pay depositors, a constraint not found in the
British banking system. So the money market mutual funds
began to siphon off deposits that would ordinarily have been
kept in a commercial bank or savings and loan association
(building society). The effect was quite dramatic as the funds
grew to sizeable amounts. A conservative estimate of their size
by year end 1985 was about $220 billion. Table 2.1 shows the
growth of the money funds in recent years. This disintermediation put severe pressure on banks' sources of funds and forced
many to fund themselves in other ways, the CD market being
one prime example. Eventually, legislation was passed to
phase-out interest rate ceilings on bank account products so
that banks and other depository institutions could compete
with this new interest rate environment.[8]

In 1980, the Depository Institutions Deregulation and Monetary Control Act was passed by Congress. It charged the
Depository Institutions Deregulation Committee (DIDC) with
implementing an orderly phase-out of interest rate ceilings over
a six year period, ending at the end of March, 1986. Adopting a
stage by stage approach, the DIDC enabled banks to compete

TABLE 2.1   Money market mutual funds outstanding in the United States

Year	Amount outstanding ($ billions)*
1982 (Dec)	236.3
1983 (Dec)	181.4
1984 (Dec)	230.2
1985 (Dec)	241.1
1986 (Feb)	248.1

*Includes general purpose funds and institutional funds
SOURCE: *Federal Reserve Bulletin*, May 1986

with money market funds and other new interest rate sensitive instruments in order to retain their source of funds.

The way in which funds are diverted by money market mutual funds provides a classic example of the disintermediation process upon commercial banks. When the individual invests in a fund, he either withdraws money from a more traditional bank account or diverts funds ordinarily intended for such an account. The bank now has less low-yielding deposits to lend out at commercial rates. So the bank's funding base can suffer a cutback in growth as well as its profit margins. The increased costs of funding also narrows the spread between the rate of the liability (deposit) as opposed to the rate received on the loan. As mentioned earlier, loans are a bank's major assets so if they become less profitable the bank's balance sheet will suffer as a result. And in a competitive world, banks will seek to make loans since it is one of the major measures of their relative sizes (see Tables 2.2 and 2.3). If they seeks higher profit margins due to the increased costs of funds, many will ultimately seek out riskier loans at higher rates of interest than the return on their more traditional portfolio.

The mutual fund, on the other hand, uses the monies invested in it to purchase money market instruments such as Treasury bills, commercial paper, and bank CDs, charging a small spread for its service. This buying power by the funds, when taken in aggregate, has made them some of the largest investors

TABLE 2.2   Ten largest American banks, by assets, as of 31 December 1984

Bank	Assets ($ 000)	Loans ($ 000)
Citicorp	150 586 000	102 707 000
BankAmerica Corp.	117 679 502	84 043 461
Chase Manhattan Corp.	86 883 018	61 341 947
Manufacturers Hanover Corp.	75 713 707	57 580 748
J. P. Morgan & Co.	64 136 000	35 239 000
Chemical New York Corp.	52 236 326	36 881 590
Security Pacific Corp.	46 117 443	32 491 663
First Interstate Bancorp.	45 543 000	28 567 464
Bankers Trust New York Corp.	45 208 147	22 148 662
First Chicago Corp.	39 845 731	25 284 052

SOURCE: *Fortune*, June 1985

TABLE 2.3   Ten largest banks outside the United States, by assets, as of 31 December 1983

Bank (Country)	Assets*	Loans*
Dai-Ichi Kangyo Bank (Japan)	116 639 338	67 821 265
Fuji Bank (Japan)	108 495 018	57 771 076
Sumitomo Bank (Japan)	105 565 992	55 645 945
Mitsubishi Bank (Japan)	101 475 349	54 354 309
Banque Nationale de Paris (Fr.)	101 170 644	81 109 454
Sanwa Bank (Japan)	95 440 356	53 686 510
Barclays Bank (UK)	94 208 156	82 824 041
Caisse Nationale de Credit Agricole (Fr.)	90 346 695	51 413 149
Credit Lyonnais (Fr.)	88 255 516	70 661 518
National Westminster Bank (UK)	87 114 675	77 221 251

*In US dollar equivalents
SOURCE: *Fortune*, August 1984

in the money markets on behalf of their individual as well as institutional clients. The major difference in economic function that has occurred is simple; the fund has siphoned off some of the money traditionally destined for a bank. As a result, banks will in some cases be forced to fund through the money market where the same funds will be willing to buy these short-term obligations at the prevailing rates. So the bank is now paying more for its funds, the money market mutual funds profit, and the investor also receives a higher rate of interest than the bank was originally able to offer.

Because of this disintermediation process, many banks have diversified their lending bases and actively sought out assets yielding more than the traditional prime rate based commercial loan. And if the DIDC achieves its goals in the long run, they will be able to offer more instruments in order to compete. But the one net effect most pronounced is that the older form of deposit account paying minimal interest, regardless of money market conditions, fell quickly by the financial wayside.

In Britain, this type of direct bank competition has not been much in evidence due to the fact that British deposit rates are able to float with the lending rates of banks, with no effective ceilings. This has meant that money was prone to remain in the banks rather than go roaming for higher yields unless they were significantly higher. Money market type funds do exist but on a smaller scale than in the United States. However, as the financial services sector continues to grow and expand into areas traditionally serviced by banks the effect will undoubtedly begin to mushroom. More will be said concerning this process and how it has effected other depository institutions on both sides of the Atlantic in Chapter 4.

NOTES

1. The London clearing banks include Barclays, National Westminster, Lloyds, Midland, Coutts, and Williams & Glyn's.
2. This syndication process is similar to the underwriting of a bond or equity offering in that the arranger of the deal is called the lead manager while the other participating banks are known as (partial) underwriters. The major difference between the two methods lies in the way risk is spread among underwriters. In security offerings, underwriters sell on their participations to the investing public. In syndicated loan offerings, the bank books the participation as a loan, or asset, on its balance sheet.
3. A discount rate can vary from country to country, depending upon banking practices. In the United States, the discount rate is the rate the Federal Reserve charges banks to borrow required reserves at the discount window. On a day-to-day basis, most banks requiring reserves will in fact borrow them from other banks in the federal funds market.
4. The Fed's actions in the marketplace are closely monitored by the investment community both in America and abroad. Since the actions of its market policy-making group, the Open Market Committee, are not made public until about a month after it meets every five weeks, 'Fed watching' has become a preoccupation in the marketplace.
5. The Fed occasionally purchases bonds in the marketplace through what is known as a 'coupon pass'. This means that if the Fed purchases, the bonds and their interest, will not be available to the investing public.
6. Call money and federal funds have a common trait in that both may be tightened without recourse to official policy actions by the central bank.
7. The Scottish clearing banks include the Bank of Scotland, Royal Bank of Scotland, and Clydesdale Bank.
8. Prior to the passing of the Depository Institutions Deregulation and Monetary Control Act, bank accounts were strictly limited in the amount of interest they could pay. The exception to the rule was made for thrift institutions (S&Ls and savings banks) that were allowed to pay one quarter of 1 per cent more than the commercial banks.

3 Investment Banking

Except in those countries where universal banking is practised, the structure and functions of investment banking are usually separate from commercial banking. The term 'investment banking' is almost as broad as commercial banking in that it encompasses many specialised functions under one generic umbrella. But regardless of where it is practised, investment banking is nevertheless an activity that is directly related to securities and securities markets.

This form of banking grew out of the commercial practices of the nineteenth century when specialised finance houses aided in trade-related or entrepreneurial business for either a fee or an equity stake in the venture itself. By its very nature, it assumes risks that many times are too great for a commercial bank to handle because of institutional or regulatory constraints. At the same time, its method of compensation was and is also different from that of a commercial bank or similar depository institution. Rather than perform a banking function for a flat fee or interest rate spread, investment banks normally negotiate fees with clients; the price being contingent upon risk and capital employed.

Traditionally, investment banking has been most closely identified with the issue of securities; that is, extending capital to a company by acting either as agent or as principal for its debt or equity issues. This is still the major focus of the industry worldwide. But it also includes other functions that may vary from country to country. In Britain, investment banking is referred to as merchant banking: that is, providing specialised services and advice to corporations and governments while usually not employing much of the firm's own capital. While this is almost similar to the functions of American investment banks, it includes one other ability not found in the United

States – the ability to take deposits. As will be seen in this chapter, British merchant banks also classify as depository institutions.

Apart from historical and some functional differences, many American investment banks are striving to become merchant banking oriented while many British merchant banks are gearing themselves up to become more powerful in the securities business by expanding their capital bases as their American counterparts have done. The financial services revolution mentioned in the previous chapter on commercial banking has an investment banking parallel, in that, besides creating many of these new instruments that have provided competition for commercial banks, the investment banks have been responsible for 'internationalising' the securities markets worldwide. In order to do so, they have required additional capital and extended facilities in the major capital markets. By broadening their product bases and trading operations, many have now become truly 'internationalised' themselves and their dissimilar functions are beginning to fuse together.

Much of the effectiveness of investment banking has to do with what is known as 'placing power' – the ability to underwrite risk securities and then sell them on to investment clients for a fee. Usually this ability is most directly linked to securities markets where certain investment banks, because of substantial client contacts, are able to sell new issues of stocks and/or bonds to clients of long or close standing. In more traditional merchant banking, however, the ability is still evident but more often seen in private transactions, where the intermediary will bring two clients together in order to initiate and complete a transaction. Knowledge of both the markets and specific client needs are in fact placing power to a merchant bank, even if it does not always involve itself in the securities markets.

One of the major differences between an investment bank and a commercial bank is the structure of their respective customer bases. Commercial banks owe their *raison d' etre* to their customers' deposits. As lenders of money they have a different relationship with their customers from that of an investment bank which relies upon market timing and specialised fees rather than upon a captive source of loanable funds.

Since investment banks do not deal with the public, their intermediary function is viewed in market terms as agents between corporate, governmental, or quasi-governmental bodies and the institutional investing public. While all financial institutions are subject to market related forces, especially changes in interest rates, investment banks are especially susceptible since they are exposed to rates that constantly change rather than to fixed rates, even for short periods of time. This is true both for their underwriting functions as well as in their trading functions in both equity and fixed income markets. Their profits depend entirely, in these instances, upon selling a security at a price higher than that at which they underwrote it. In short, their banking function as such is by its nature more volatile and risky than the commercial banking function although it should not be implied that the latter is a risk-free activity; the comparison of the two in general terms only serves to illustrate that the nature of banking risk varies considerably.

AMERICAN INVESTMENT BANKING

Organisationally, American investment banking is broken down along geographical or regional lines. At the local level, investment banks operate in certain states or regions where they can best serve their client base; underwriting securities for local companies and municipal authorities. Their activities are complemented, and often superseded, by those banks with national offices and interests, most often located in the major money centres where the major commercial banks are also found.

The nationally organised investment bank will extend its underwriting and trading capabilities to securities of all sectors of the national economy: from debt obligations of the federal government and its various agencies to debt of state and local governments and to debt and equity issues of corporate entities.

In the most contemporary sense, investment banking involves both the underwriting of securities and the maintaining of a secondary market in many of them, especially if they are bonds or equities listed over the counter. This trading function is also known as the 'market making' function. Prior to the 1970s, it was possible for some long established investment banks to underwrite securities (primarily bonds in this case) and not trade them afterwards. But due to the changing nature of the marketplace and the move toward a full service investment banking function, most major underwriters eventually entered the trading markets as well.

Even though investment banking now includes both elements in its business it is still not the same as a brokerage function in the strict sense of the word. It is possible to perform the two major functions without being a broker; conversely it is possible to be a broker without being an investment banker. More will be said concerning this in a later section in this chapter.

The original mainstay of investment banking is securities underwriting. As has already been mentioned, the one part of this function that remains the sole preserve of investment banks is the underwriting of corporate securities – either stocks or bonds. Other types of bonds (government, agency or municipal) may be underwritten by commercial banks, but again, it is the investment banks' expertise that sets them in the forefront of the business.

Underwriting is a process whereby the risk of providing funds for a borrower or seller of equity in securities form is syndicated among members of the investment banking community rather than taken on by one institution itself. Because of their relatively small capital bases, underwriters are not apt to take on the entire risk of a new security issue but will sell a portion of it to other underwriters in turn.

An example of how this process works illustrates the attempt to spread out risk. Assume for a moment that a company decides to raise capital through an equity issue of 10 million shares. The shares will be priced and the issue will have a dollar value.[1] If the shares are priced at $20 then the value of the issue will be $200 million.

The underwriting process means that the investment banks will put up the cash for the issue with the company receiving the proceeds, less negotiated commissions. The next stage in the process is for the lead investment bank to sell the shares to the investing public. But it is at this juncture that the risk in this process becomes evident. The time that the securities remain in the hands of the underwriter exposes it to market risk. If the shares should fall in price because of weak demand or other market conditions, the underwriter takes the loss. Conversely, if the shares should rise above their new issue price the profit will be taken by the underwriter as well. The company receives the value of the shares times the amount of shares sold; again referring back, $200 million less commissions.

Because the underwriter would have to carry the full value of the shares on its books, it will form an underwriting syndicate and sell off pieces of the original amount to other investment banks. Each bank is responsible financially for the shares it subscribes to. So in addition to spreading the risk to other institutions, the original investment bank will also now be faced with additional competition in that these other banks will also be offering securities to the public. But allowing others into the issue is the price the lead underwriter is most often willing to pay for a diminished capital risk.

This syndication method has also been adopted by some commercial banks when granting large loans. These 'jumbo' loans may be too large for any one single institution to take on and syndication becomes an effective method of alleviating pressure. But here the similarity between the two methods ends; in commercial banking the loan is held in the banks' portfolios as an asset and has a direct bearing upon profit margins. In investment banking, the syndication period is used for selling the securities on to the public. The risk ends for the investment banks when the securities are sold; they become assets of the buyers, not the underwriters.

Although there are many variations of underwriting, this is the general process they all follow regardless of whether they are issues of shares or bonds. Because of volatile markets in recent years, even such deals as private placements have been syndicated rather than being initially held by only one underwriting bank.[2]

Following underwriting, some of the banks involved will endeavour to make a market in the securities. This means that they will be one of several investment banks maintaining an inventory of that particular security and quote two-way prices (bid-offer) on it for those interested in trading. In this case, market-making means exactly what the term implies.

It should be noted that this function applies to all types of bonds and to over-the-counter stocks or if the bank endeavours to make a market in listed shares in what is known as the fourth market; that is, trading large blocks of listed shares away from their residual stock exchange. But it should not automatically be assumed that underwriters make markets in all issues they participate in. Quite to the contrary; the process by which an issue is chosen to trade can be quite selective and ultimately centres around questions such as the issue's potential popularity, liquidity and investor interest.

One of the intangible, but nevertheless significant, aspects of investment banking has been its contribution to financial innovation. While difficult to measure, the impact is considerable. Many of the techniques applied in modern capital markets have originated from this sector. The main reason investment banks have been so successful in this respect can be attributed to the unique niche in the marketplace that they have carved for themselves. As both underwriters and sellers of securities they are in a strong position to tailor capital market instruments to the needs of their clients. Usually, the more successful of the banks have been the larger institutions utilising their national and international offices and contacts for maximum gain. The largest of the American investment banks can be found in Table 3.1.

Using their intermediary role effectively, investment banks have been in the forefront of developing various types of options on both fixed income securities and foreign exchange, bonds with variable rates of interest, convertible options, morgage-backed (collateralised) securities, asset-backed fixed income obligations, and variable-rate preferred stocks among

TABLE 3.1 Ten largest American investment banks/brokers, by capitalisation

Firm	Total capital ($ 000)
Salomon Brothers	2 315 287
Shearson Lehman Brothers	2 251 000
Merrill Lynch	2 169 521
Prudential-Bache	1 259 260
Goldman, Sachs	1 201 000
First Boston	1 042 200
Drexel Burnham Lambert	958 250
Dean Witter Reynolds	884 030
Bear Stearns	800 000
E. F. Hutton	755 998

SOURCE: *Institutional Investor*, April 1986

others. In many cases, the basic concept behind these types of securities or secondary market trading vehicles has been imported from the European markets via the euromarkets where many of the banks are also active. The variable rate of interest as applied to bonds or preferred stock is but one example. In addition, interest rate swaps, an idea often usually associated with commercial banks that often guaranty them, also originated with the investment banks. Normally, they bring together two parties, one with fixed rate debt and the other with variable or floating rate debt, and then work out the terms of the transaction for a fee.[3]

The British equivalent of the investment bank follows along the same lines but does have significant variations in that it is subject to the jurisdiction of the Bank of England while its American counterpart is subject to the jurisdiction of the Securities and Exchange Commission (SEC) which oversees securities market operators but not depository institutions.

BRITISH MERCHANT BANKING

British merchant banking is therefore a somewhat broader activity than investment banking in the American sense. Merchant banks have existed since the early eighteenth century and have developed unique banking functions in addition to securities underwriting. The most notable of these is the ability to take deposits; a characteristic that crosses the traditional American lines but falls short of the universal banking function as described in the previous chapter.

In Britain, merchant banking developed differently from commercial banking over the years because of structural differences in the marketplace rather than because of a strictly controlled legal environment. Merchant banks developed to service the wholesale, or merchant, market rather than to deal with the retail depositor. As a result, the nature of their assets and liabilities differs from those of a clearing bank. Most important to their central function, however, is their ability to accept commercial bills (short-term money market paper) which earns them their other familiar name, accepting houses.

Strictly speaking, not all merchant banks are accepting houses but since most of them are generalisations can be safely

TABLE 3.2   Members of the Accepting Houses Committee (as of May 1986)

Brown Shipley
Charterhouse Japhet
Robert Fleming
Guiness Mahon
Hambros Bank
Hill Samuel
Morgan Grenfell

made. Technically, an accepting house accepts a bill of exchange and attaches its own guaranty of repayment to it. These bills are bought and sold on a discount basis (less than redemption value) in the secondary money market, or discount market, and can be equally discounted at the Bank of England if acceptable. The accepting houses charge a fee for their guarantees on bills since that guaranty is what the market values when trading the particular instrument.

The largest accepting houses are members of the Accepting Houses Committee which deals with matters of mutual interest and self-regulation (see Table 3.2). The central role that they play in the City of London is underscored by the fact that the Bank of England has traditionally been wary of allowing them to be taken over by foreign banking entities, although this reluctance is slowly beginning to crumble as the financial services revolution gains momentum and traditional domestic boundaries become more international in scope.

Merchant banking is probably more correctly defined as wholesale banking, but not without some reservations. Their wholesale function is not as broad as that of a truly wholesale commercial bank dealing only with institutional clients. But there are similarities. The merchant banks are able to perform a limited commercial banking function without the benefit of a retail deposit base. Without the base, they rely upon large time deposits and CDs as their primary sources of funds and similarly fund their asset base in the institutional side of the market as well; namely through loans and investments.

On the loan side, the merchant banks have been involved in a large number of syndicated loans which in their entirety would be too large for any one of them to book as an asset. Many times, they can be found in tombstone ads as the arrangers (managers) of syndicated loans with the actual funds being provided by other institutions; a position that attests to their advisory and organisational skills.

Although the merchant banks are a powerful force in British finance, their total assets represent less than about 10 per cent of that of the banking system as a whole. It is their skills and expertise that keep them in the forefront of financial innovation. This can best be measured by their success in fund management for both sterling and foreign currency investments.

The larger of the merchant banks are also some of Britain's largest fund managers, overseeing institutional and individual investment portfolios. The majority of these funds under management are sterling denominated gilt-edged government bonds or London traded equities. But the merchants have also been responsible for a good deal of financial innovation in packaging investment products for both domestic and international consumption. Among their innovations have been international bond and money market funds, foreign currency funds, and investment trusts (mutual funds) made up solely of equity investments in foreign stock markets.

On the American-style investment banking front, the merchant banks double as issuing houses, bringing new issues of corporate securities (almost exclusively stocks) to market. Since the British corporate bond market has been moribund for the last twenty years, little issuing activity has been seen and most new issues come in equity form. New issues have been almost entirely underwritten by the merchant banks although the clearing banks have made some inroads in recent years. There is no legislation present to prevent them from doing so if they desire.

In addition to UK securities, many merchant banks have been active underwriters of bonds in the euromarket where underwriting techniques are quite similar to those used in the American capital market. While the methods of new share issuance differ from American practice, this area of international bond underwriting is one sector that has enabled the marketplace to become truly international, and somewhat standard in terms of underwriting techniques and even fee structures.

So while the merchant banks are deposit takers and are

recognised as such by the Bank of England, their activities as wholesale institutions extend beyond the traditional banking function for industry into being active money market participants as well as underwriters of corporate securities and fund managers. However, the distinction between issuing house and broker, often combined in the United States, is kept separated in Britain, again for traditional reasons rather than for reasons of regulation.

STOCKBROKERAGE

Brokerage, or broking, is a function performed by a financial intermediary that may be an investment bank, or more simply, just a stockbroker with no other institutional affiliations. In the United States, most stockbrokers are now also investment bankers; the brokerage function being nothing more than an outlet for new issues underwritten by the firm. But in its pure sense, broking need not be identified with any other sort of financial intermediary function. The most simple definition of it is that it is the ability to bring together buyer and seller of a security in a secondary market, charging a fee or commission for the service.

While this definition is fairly simple, the practical aspects of broking are somewhat more difficult to outline. Brokerage involves executing orders on the behalf of clients, using the stockbroker's access to the floor of a securities exchange, an ability not available to the general public. For this service, the broker charges a fee prorated on the size of the transaction. The actual amount of fees, or commissions, is the subject of intense competition within the brokerage industry and has led to widespread changes in the structure of the industry itself.

In practice, brokerage is an oligopolistic industry in that its practices, while being fairly standard, are executed by a relatively small group of firms, belonging to a self-regulating body overseeing the industry. Most often it is confused with the market making function performed by investment banks. This is perhaps the most common source of confusion about the industry, especially as understood by laymen. Brokerage is not only a function of those who buy and sell stocks on behalf of the investing public; it is also a function found in the wholesale money markets, foreign exchange markets, and bond markets. Essentially, a broker is one who brings together buyers and sellers; the broker will buy from the seller and sell to the buyer only if both parties agree to the terms. He will not buy for his own account and then seek someone to sell to in turn. If he does in fact perform this latter function he is acting as agent and principal, not simply as a broker. A broker's role is viewed as less risky; all he does is match orders, taking a fraction of the price for his service.

In the over-the-counter markets the brokerage function can prove quite valuable since buyers and sellers are often disbursed over wide geographical areas. A broker may know of a potential buyer who is unknown to the seller and the broker's ability to manoeuvre between the two can be useful. In central auction markets, such as the major stock exchanges, the function is the same, although performed in a different, and more familiar, fashion.

Brokers regularly take orders from customers and pass them to their agents on the floor of the stock exchange. The agent then executes them with the particular market maker for each security.[4] The actual transaction risk lies with the market maker on the floor, not with the broker.

Virtually all stock exchange transactions are executed by stockbrokers on behalf of the public except for those very large transactions sometimes executed by an investment bank directly between customers, called a block trade in the United States and a pass-through in Britain. The investment banking link comes when brokers who are also attached to a particular investment bank execute the order away from an exchange.

The role of the broker is more clearly seen in the United States on a retail level than it is in Britain due to differences in the investing public. About 25 per cent of all stock exchange turnover in America is attributed to the retail investor, the balance being invested by institutions. In Britain, the retail element is smaller due to differences in per capita income. Also, unit trusts are popular in Britain among the retail investors and account for a high percentage of individuals' funds placed in the market. But the purchasing power of unit trusts is not retail but institutional in nature, since it is the unit trust management company that does the actual stock selection and buying and selling.

Large American investment banks have brokerage facilities attached to them in order to provide an effective outlet for their underwritings not sold to institutional investors. In this case, brokerage is an adjunct capability of investment banking in that the broker is selling a new issue rather than acting as an intermediary in the secondary market. But as Table 3.1 illustrates, the largest American investment banks are also brokers by current definition.

Another important role of brokers is the agency function they perform between individuals and investment products such as mutual funds or money market funds. In this instance, the broker is not executing a stock, bond, option, or commodity futures trade but is buying or selling an institutional investment to the individual. The purchase of a share of a mutual fund or unit trust represents ownership in the fund which is in turn based upon a specific sort of investment with a specific goal in mind. In this situation, brokers act as agents of the fund rather than of a stock exchange.

INVESTMENT BANKING, STOCKBROKING AND THE FINANCIAL SERVICES REVOLUTION

Investment banking and stockbroking have been at the centre of the financial services revolution that has developed since the early 1980s in the United States and Britain. This rapid change of events has been prompted by deregulation within the securities industry generally, enabling many banks, other non-bank financial intermediaries, and corporations to form associations aimed at providing more than one specialised service from under one roof.

Perhaps the most powerful, single force in the centralisation of the securities industry has been the abandonment of fixed commissions on stock exchange transactions in favour of negotiated commissions. While this would appear, at first glance, to be an important factor, it would not immediately appear to be a catalyst. However, it was the change in commission structure that rationalised the American securities industry and the proposal to abolish fixed commissions that did the same for the British side of the industry.

Negotiated commissions means that a broker and his client

agree on a commission rather than the broker charging the client a flat fee pro-rated upon the size of the transaction itself. This effectively benefits those clients doing the most active trading; it has a lesser effect upon the small, retail trader. In this sort of competitive environment, the broker charging the least will be able to lure customers away from others if its services are otherwise competitive.

Fixed commissions were abolished in the American market in May 1975. In the decade following, many small brokerage houses disappeared from the investment scene, either having merged with larger houses that absorbed their client bases or in some cases having gone out of business entirely. The abolition of the fixed charges simply meant that many of the small houses were unable to compete with the facilities offered by the larger ones.

The British market followed some eleven years later, with fixed commissions abolished in the autumn of 1986. Rather than phase-out the fixed schedule over time, the London Stock Exchange abolished them all at once in favour of negotiated rates, precipitating what has become popularly known as the 'Big Bang' in the London market. However, it was the New York example that ultimately led to the demise of fixed rates in London.

Because of the structural differences between the two markets, plus the added disincentive of the British stamp tax (a government-levied tax on stock exchange turnover), it became cheaper for some London institutions to trade London listed shares in New York rather than on their own exchange. That sort of aberration led to increased commissions for New York brokers or London brokers with New York affiliates. Ultimately, it showed the imperfections in the UK system and negotiated commissions were introduced.

Merely the suggestion of negotiated commissions began a series of mergers, acquisitions and an overall rationalisation of the London securities market. Many small-and medium-sized stockbrokers were bought up by larger institutions. And these acquirers were not all other stockbrokers; in many cases they were commercial banks, merchant banks and foreign institutions as well. The motivating force behind this centralisation was simple; only the larger institutions would be able to compete with the more highly capitalised American and foreign institutions. But at this juncture, the motivation was now also international, not purely domestic.

Another aspect of the financial services revolution has been its international element. With the growth in the euromarkets, and the eurobond market in particular, it became obvious that only large firms with international dealing capabilities would be able to survive an environment that had become truly 'internationalised' in character. This new element extended beyond eurobonds: because of the change in international tax laws and the innovations in information services it was now possible to trade many investment instruments in more than one market around the world. For instance, while the largest market for US government bonds is obviously within the United States, a large number are also traded in London before the beginning of daily business in New York. Many of the market makers in the bonds are the same as in New York: those investment banks and others characterised as primary securities dealers. Only their location changed. Rather than only making prices from New York or elsewhere within the United States, the same group began quoting and trading them in London, in order to serve those clients in different time zones.

The securities houses were not totally responsible for the internationalisation of the securities markets. In many cases, they were very quick to react to changes brought about by shifts in the international investment climate. For instance, when the United States abolished its withholding tax, traditionally levied on foreign holders of American securities in 1984, the West German government was quick to follow suit. Although the Americans abolished the tax to encourage more indirect (portfolio) foreign investment in the face of an enormous budget deficit, the Germans followed suit for a different reason. Rather than suffer a lack of demand in their own domestic markets caused by a shift in investor preferences because of the difference in taxes, they abolished them in order to ensure a continued, orderly flow of international capital into the German bond, and to a lesser extent, stock markets.[5]

But regardless of the original source of this internationalisation, it was nevertheless the investment banks/brokers that facilitated cross-market trading and made continuous trading of securities a reality. It was this expanded trading ability that also led to expanded financial products.

As mentioned earlier, the investment banks have been in the forefront of financial product innovation. Because of their specialised expertise plus international contacts they have been able to devise new instruments drawing upon concepts from one market and introducing them into another. The sole motivation behind this phenomenon has been profit; the assumption being that new financial products will foster increased trading in them and in related products. For instance, by devising options traded on fixed income instruments such as bonds, the investment bank is able to benefit both from the trading of the actual bonds themselves as well as on the options.[6] On the client side, the investor is offered a means whereby risk can be mitigated by the sale or purchase of the option. Similarly, the floating or adjustable rate bond (where the interest payment is re-set periodically above a money market rate) enables the investment bank to charge an underwriting fee for issuing it, and developing a trading capacity in this specialised instrument also leading to potential profitability. The investment client gains by purchasing an instrument that is designed not to suffer capital loss because it is periodically set at the prevailing rate of interest. The borrower benefits by potentially lowering its cost of capital by avoiding fixed charges over the life of the bond.

This innovative spirit plus the ability to adapt to changing market conditions is the quality that makes investment banks potential merger targets by larger firms such as commercial banks or insurance companies; institutions that are sometimes slow to react to market changes because of their sheer size or restrictive regulatory environment. The ability to show a profit under different market conditions makes them attractive to those other financial intermediaries which, by virtue of size or institutional contraints, are not by themselves quite as flexible.

NOTES

1. For a further explanation of this process see Charles R. Geisst, *A Guide to the Financial Markets* (London: Macmillan; New York: St Martin's Press, 1982), Chapter 1.
2. A private placement is essentially a bond issue not registered with the Securities & Exchange Commission. It is underwritten by an investment bank, commercial bank, or merchant bank and sold to a small group of

investors that normally holds the obligation until maturity. These instruments normally do not have a secondary market value.

3. An interest rate swap, where an agent brings together two borrowers, involves the swapping of a floating rate of interest for a fixed rate of interest so that both borrowers benefit by obtaining lower than market rates. The actual swap transaction is guaranteed by commercial banks and booked as an off balance sheet liability, also called a contingent liability.

4. The market maker on the floor of American stock exchanges is called a specialist. It is he who conducts the auction market for a special group of stocks that he trades exclusively.

5. Capital flows between countries are a major source of both direct and indirect foreign investment. In the indirect, or portfolio, investment sense simple mechanical regulations such as withholding taxes on forigners holding domestic securities can often impede a domestic market's ability to raise funds.

6. In theory, derivative products such as options or futures on financial instruments tend to enhance the trading of the financial assets upon which they are based. If a shareholder knows that he will be able to use options to hedge his holdings or enhance their return, he is more apt to hold those stocks rather than abandon them because of increased risk or diminished returns.

4 Building Associations

The title of this chapter is something of a hybrid; it reflects a joint, coined name to describe British building societies and their American counterparts, savings and loan associations (S&Ls). Both of these institutions have a common function within their respective economies that has not changed substantially in the last hundred years – both channel savers' funds into the mortgage or real estate market. And while this purpose may have begun to vary due to current monetary deregulation and financial innovation, building associations have carved out a large, almost monopolistic niche in the financial services sector which will probably remain entrenched, despite increasing competition from the commercial banks.

Of the two institutions, the British is older by about fifty years. Building societies first sprang up in Birmingham and then spread to other parts of the English Midlands toward the last quarter of the eighteenth century. Their original purpose was to pool together members' funds, originally the monies of artisans or others with similar social status and ambitions, in order to purchase land and finance home building. Organisationally, they were at first 'mutual' societies in that they were owned by their members; that is, by their depositors.

The first American building association was established in Philadelphia in 1831 and was called the Oxford Provident Building Association, constituted almost exactly on the English model. It too was a mutual society in that it provided a pool of funds from which members could borrow in order to finance a home on a mutual basis. In this respect, American S&Ls have not changed substantially since their early days. By year end 1984, some 80 per cent were still organised as mutual associations while the remainder were organised as stock companies; that is, owned by shareholders.

Despite their common origins and characteristics, British and American building associations have developed several quite distinct operational differences over the years which have only recently begun to converge. Perhaps the most important of these is the reliance upon floating, or adjustable, interest rates as the basis for accepting deposits and for pricing new mortgages. While this has been the British practice for the last generation, American S&Ls have only recently begun to adopt adjustable rates as the basis for their interest rate setting policies. More will be said concerning this topic in a section below.

Savings and loans and building societies were once the major, and sometimes only, sources of money borrowed for home purchases. Today they face increasing pressure from commercial banks in both countries which have borrowed many of the societies' methods of pricing mortgages. And while the traditional source of funds for both remains essentially the same, large commercial banks have been able to tap a source of funds in the capital markets many times not available to the smaller building associations because of their lack of stature in the markets.

The competition provided by other depository institutions has forced many building associations to change some of their traditional practices. For instance, it is no longer mandatory for a customer to have funds on deposit with a society before applying for a mortgage. The older practice that dictated that societies only actually lent to their own depositors, a type of compensating balance, has in many cases fallen by the wayside in favour of more contemporary, competitive practices. While it is still appropriate to say that the societies survive in much of their original forms, their actual lending and depository practices have in fact changed due to increasing external pressures from other sectors of the financial industry.

ORGANISATION AND GENERAL PURPOSES

The structural organisations of S&Ls and building societies is very similar to that of commercial banks in both the United States and Britain. In America, S&Ls are chartered either by the state in which they reside or by the federal government through one of its agencies. In Britain, all financial institutions ultimately fall under the aegis of the Bank of England.

At year end 1984, 3391 S&Ls existed in the United States. While the number appears somewhat large, the state of the economy and the housing market drastically reduced the number from previous years. In 1960, over 6300 S&Ls existed, dwindling to slightly over 4000 in 1975. The most drastic rationalisation came in the relatively short period between 1980 and 1984 when the number again fell from 4292 to 3391.[1] Of this most recent figure, about 50 per cent of the associations were federally chartered, with the balance being chartered by their respective states.

The federally chartered associations are subject to the supervision of the Federal Home Loan Bank Board, itself a federal agency, that sets down standards for chartering new associations, sets operating procedures, and supervises the types of loans made. By virtue of the fact that 50 per cent of S&Ls are federally chartered, they are also automatically members of the Federal Savings and Loan Insurance Corporation (FSLIC), the S&L counterpart of the Federal Deposit Insurance Corporation (FDIC), mentioned in Chapter 2. FSLIC insures depositors' funds up to a current maximum of $100 000; the same level of insurance provided by FDIC. The majority of state chartered S&Ls also belong to FSLIC on a voluntary basis although they are not obligated to do so. All institutional members of FSLIC, as their commercial banking counterparts in FDIC, pay a premium to FSLIC in order to provide coverage for their depositors.

In America, S&Ls are organised as either stock companies or mutual associations, the classic model. A stock company, as any other publicly-held corporation, issues capital stock held by shareholders and is traded on a stock exchange or in the over-the-counter market. A mutual association does not issue capital stock but is owned by its depositors, who are entitled to vote on business issues in much the same way that a stockholder would in a publicly-held company. The British experience has tended toward stock companies, despite the historical origins of the building societies, regardless of the size of the building society itself.

The major purpose of building associations continues to be the directing of savings deposits, their major source of funds, into the real estate market, as loans for residences. In order to attract these funds, building associations offer a number of accounts, ranging from checking (current) accounts to term deposits or a combination of the two; that is, accounts providing both checking facilities that also bear a rate of interest. But in most cases, the accounts offered are short-term in nature. Because of this traditional structure, S&Ls in the United States have been forced to restructure the interest rates on their mortgages outstanding so that a serious mismatching does not occur, especially in times of interest rate volatility.

Regardless of the organisation of the capital structure of building associations, the fact that they are depository institutions means that depositors have first claim upon assets in the event of liquidation. In a mutual company this distinction is somewhat superfluous because no capital stock exists although in a stock company it is the depositor (as creditor) who is entitled to the same right before any stockholder distributions are made.

American S&Ls recently have become more diversified than their British counterparts in terms of lending to borrowers for loans other than mortgages. While British building societies tend to restrict themselves almost exclusively to home mortgages, S&Ls do make loans for automobile purchases, consumer durables, and, in some cases, issue credit cards and offer trust services. This broadening of their asset product base is intended to make them more diversified and less susceptible to the vagaries of the housing market and its attendant interest rate problems. As a result, their reserve requirements now are similar to those imposed upon American commercial banks engaging in many of the same activities.

RESERVE REQUIREMENTS

American savings and loans are subject to liquidity requirements as set down by the Federal Home Loan Bank Board. This body sets regulations for federally chartered institutions only; those chartered by their respective states are subject to levels mandated by state banking authorities. The Bank Board is currently empowered to vary the liquidity ratios of its member institutions between 4 and 10 per cent of the size of savings accounts and other borrowings due within one year or less.

Specifically, there are two types of reserve levels, liability reserves and asset reserves. On the liability side, funds are set aside to protect depositors against loan or investment loss in the institutions' portfolios. Under normal circumstances, these reserves represent net worth: the amount by which assets exceed liabilities on the S&L balance sheet.

Asset reserves, on the other hand, are set aside against deposits in order to ensure some liquidity in the event that depositors begin to withdraw funds propitiously at any given point in time. This form of reserve is similar to primary reserves of a commercial bank in that they must be held as cash, both at the Federal Reserve Bank and at the S&Ls themselves. Since 1980, S&Ls have been subject to the same asset reserve requirements as commercial banks and all other depository institutions as set down by the 1980 deregulation act.

British building societies' reserve requirements are dictated by the Authorisation Regulations. Essentially, reserve levels held will depend upon the size of a building society's total assets, with the smaller societies having a minimum reserve ratio of $2\frac{1}{2}$ per cent while the largest hold about 1.3 per cent. Thus, there is a sliding scale upward as the size of the society diminishes. In terms of liquidity, there is no special level of liquid funds mandated, although legislation holds that a society must keep $7\frac{1}{2}$ per cent of its total assets liquid; however most generally maintain liquidity at higher levels. Tradition plays a role in determining the exact amount that societies will actually hold, either in cash or marketable (usually government or government-backed) securities. For instance, when the ratio of withdrawals to receipts measures an increase, societies will obviously ensure that liquidity is on hand to meet anticipated demand for cash. If the ratio tapers off, liquidity may diminish from previous levels. However, the $7\frac{1}{2}$ per cent requirement is deemed far too small for most societies so the actual level of liquidity is almost certainly at a higher multiple of the minimum.

ASSETS AND LIABILITIES

At year end 1983, savings association assets in the United

States totalled some \$771 705 million, up from \$271 905 million ten years earlier. Of the 1983 total, some \$493 432 million was classified as mortgage loans with the majority of the balance held in cash and investment securities, including mortgage backed securities guaranteed by certain federal agencies.[2] The distribution of British building society assets was similar: at year end 1984 mortgages accounted for 80 per cent of total assets with investment securities accounting for most of the balance. This comparison between the two countries can be seen in Table 4.1.

Traditionally, building associations have not been investors in corporate stocks or bonds. They chiefly confine themselves to government or government-backed debt issues. Within this latter category, American thrift institutions have more diverse

TABLE 4.1 Assets of Savings & Loan Associations and Building Societies 1980–1984

| | Savings & Loans (\$ millions) | | | |
	Total assets	Mortgages	Cash and securities	Other*
1980	629 829	502 812	57 572	69 445
1981	664 167	518 547	63 123	82 497
1982	707 646	483 614	85 438	138 594
1983	771 705	493 432	103 395	174 878
1984	na	na	na	na

*Includes real estate, FHLB stock and GNMA obligations

| | Building Societies (£ millions) | | | |
	Total assets	Mortgages	Securities	Other*
1980	54 317	42 708	5 240	6369
1981	62 147	49 039	6 459	6649
1982	74 485	57 186	9 307	7992
1983	87 190	68 114	10 559	8517
1984	101 896	82 686	11 058	8152

*Includes s-t assets, local authority obligations, offices
SOURCES: United States League of Savings Associations, *Sourcebook* 1985; Central Statistical Office, *Financial Statistics*, September 1985

instruments in which to invest than their British counterparts. They are able to invest in US Government agency bonds, paying higher interest rates than Treasury issues, while still receiving the full faith and credit backing of the government itself. Normally, S&Ls invest in obligations of the Government National Mortgage Association, the Federal Home Loan Mortgage Corporation and several other government related agencies. In the case of the Home Loan Mortgage Corporation, the obligations are backed by pools of residential mortgages, so when an S&L purchases one of these bonds it is tantamount to purchasing a tangible (real) asset and is treated as such for tax purposes.

TABLE 4.2   Liabilities of Savings & Loan Associations and Building Societies 1980–1984

		Savings & Loans ($ millions)			
	Total	Savings deposits	FHLB advances	Other*	Net worth
1980	629 829	510 959	64 491	54 379	33 391
1981	664 167	525 061	88 782	50 324	28 395
1982	707 646	567 961	97 850	41 835	26 233
1983	773 417	634 455	92 227	46 735	30 867
1984	902 449	724 301	126 169	51 979	34 764

*Includes loans in process

		Building Societies (£ millions)		
	Total	Savings deposits*	Bank borrowing†	Other‡
1980	54 317	49 950	3403	964
1981	62 147	57 146	4018	983
1982	74 485	67 661	5825	999
1983	87 190	78 225	6612	2353
1984	101 896	91 442	7798	9675

*Includes shares
†Includes negotiable bonds and reserves, official loans
‡Includes time deposits and CDs, interest accrued but not credited
SOURCES: United States League of Savings Associations, *Sourcebook* 1985;
    Central Statistical Office, *Financial Statistics*, September 1985

On the liability side, S&Ls' savings deposits are their major source of funds. Table 4.2 shows the liability breakdown of both British and American building associations. Eighty per cent of American liabilities and almost 88 per cent of British liabilities are listed as deposits (or deposits and shares in the UK case). One other category other than deposits and loans requires mention here. This is the catagory of net worth; in the most recent reporting year listed in Table 4.2 it was almost 4 per cent of the total of all US liabilities. Net worth is retained earnings and paid-in surplus as well as reserves. Net worth is listed as a liability because it represents funds not distributed, or liquidated, and as such remains a liability on an association's balance sheet.

Because of the specialised nature of the S&L and building society industry it can be seen that the asset and liability distribution is fairly straightforward when compared to larger, more diverse deposit-taking institutions such as commercial banks. In one sense, it was this narrow portfolio distribution among building associations that led to their rapid rationalisation in the late 1970s and 1980s into larger, more solvent institutions than they were previously, especially in the United States.

RATIONALISATION OF THE INDUSTRY

Earlier in this chapter, the dwindling number of building associations on both sides of the Atlantic was noted. This is not to suggest that this is a passing topic, however, because the reduced numbers does not necessarily imply that the societies have not been successful at channelling savings into the housing market. It does suggest, however, that structural changes in both the industry and the behaviour of interest rates has created a need for large, more heavily capitalised societies than ever before.

The reduction in societies on both sides of the Atlantic can be seen in Table 4.3. In the American case, the number has dwindled considerably from previous years due to the above mentioned factors plus the growing number of branches of the now larger societies. In short, the smaller associations with few,

TABLE 4.3 Number of Savings & Loan Associations and Building
Societies 1975–1984

Year	Federally chartered S&Ls	State chartered S&Ls	Building Societies
1975	2048	2883	382
1976	2019	2802	364
1977	2012	2749	339
1978	2000	2725	316
1979	1989	2695	287
1980	1985	2628	273
1981	1907	2385	253
1982	1727	2098	227
1983	1553	1949	206*
1984	1478	1913	190*

*Estimates
SOURCES: United States League of Savings Associations, *Sourcebook* 1985;
Building Societies Association, *Building Societies Yearbook, 1985*

if any, branches have fallen by the wayside in favour of larger, more highly capitalised associations represented by an expanding branch system. The major factors behind this trend will be discussed in greater detail below because they represent the primary reasons for consolidation in the financial services industry that has affected financing and borrowing trends in all of the developed capital markets.

In America the trend toward larger associations began with the spiral in interest rates that began in the mid to late 1970s. Higher rates spelled both a serious mismatch on the books of S&Ls and ultimately required government regulations designed to free financial institutions from the encumbrances that had hindered them in the old regulatory environment. But before examining this phenomenon, the more general trend toward real property investment and return among savers must be understood because it was this source of demand for funds that affected the S&Ls individually and collectively. When this demand collided with the higher interest rate regime, the effect upon the associations was almost devastating.

The growth in the demand for mortgages is closely related to the savings ratio of the population. At year end 1984, the savings ratio of the average British household was 14 per cent; that is, personal savings as a percentage of disposable income. In the United States, with a traditionally lower ratio than many other developed societies, the ratio was only 6 per cent. But despite the disparity, the return on American house prices can nevertheless be seen in Table 4.4, showing the dollar volume of new and existing one family homes sold in the United States from 1970 through to the end of 1984. It can be seen that the volume of home sales multiplied 5.7 times during that period. At the same time, the median price for new and existing homes increased by 20 per cent. While this figure does not accurately show how much a particular house grew in value over that period, it does point out that the figure is substantial enough to make home price increases compete with most financial assets in terms of compounded rates of growth.

TABLE 4.4 Dollar volume of new and existing one-family homes in the United States 1970–1984

Year	Total homes sold (000)	Dollar volume (billions)
1970	2097	54.3
1971	2674	75.1
1972	2970	89.7
1973	2968	99.3
1974	2791	101.5
1975	3025	120.0
1976	3710	160.3
1977	4469	219.0
1978	4803	272.3
1979	4536	296.6
1980	3518	258.0
1981	2855	225.6
1982	2402	194.8
1983	3342	281.8
1984	3507	309.0

SOURCE: United States League of Savings Associations. *Sourcebook*, 1985

Obviously, during this same period, the number of mortgages outstanding at both American and British building associations vacillated dramatically, as can be seen in Table 4.5. Between 1980

TABLE 4.5   Mortgages outstanding at Savings & Loan Associations and
Building Societies 1980–1984

	Savings & Loans	
	Mortgages outstanding ($ millions)	% change from previous year
1980	502 812	+ 8.7
1981	518 547	+ 3.1
1982	483 614	− 6.7
1983	493 432	+ 2.0
1984	555 277	+ 12.5

	Building Societies	
1980	42 708	+ 15.47
1981	49 039	+ 14.82
1982	57 186	+ 16.61
1983	68 114	+ 19.10
1984	82 686	+ 21.40

SOURCES: United States League of Savings Associations, *Sourcebook* 1985;
    Central Statistical Office, *Financial Statistics*, September 1985

and end 1984, American S&Ls witnessed a 2 per cent decrease
in mortgages outstanding while British building societies witnessed an astonishing 94 per cent growth rate. And it should
be noted that these figures do not include mortgages granted by
commercial banks but only by S&Ls and building societies.
This demand for mortgage money is the obvious key to the
changing housing prices in both countries.

Assume for a moment that a home purchased for 20 000 units
of currency (dollars or pounds) in 1970 was paid for with a
down payment of 20 per cent, leaving a mortgageable balance
of 16 000. This was financed for fifteen years at a fixed rate of 8
per cent interest. At the time of the final payment, the house
price had increased to 80 000: a fourfold increase.

In order to compare the actual return on the home investment, one has to take into account competitive investments and
compare their gross returns as well. Let us assume that the

safest choice the investor had at the time in financial assets was a 15 year government bond, bearing a 6 per cent rate of interest. So rather than putting the 4000 into the house, assume the investor invests in this bond.

Compounding the bond, bought at face value, on an annual basis would make the original 4000 equity worth 9586 in fifteen years, assuming no taxes paid. This represents an increase of 239.66 per cent on the original investment. The home, on the other hand, has appreciated 76 000, representing an increase of 19 times the original investment, or 1900 per cent. The actual discrepancy could be even larger than the outright comparison shown here. In order for the bond investment to grow, the interest received would have to be reinvested continuously in order to achieve the rate quoted. If this was not the case, the return would be much smaller.

Similarly, the gross return approach is not complete until taxes and opportunities are also factored in as well as inflation. The interest payments on the bond would be taxed and at the same time the investor would have to incur expenses for housing. On the other hand, the home investor will not be subject to taxes if he sells the home since it was his primary residence for those fifteen years. And the interest payments that he made were tax deductible as well; so rather than paying out for housing expense in the form of rent, for instance, he was actually able to deduct the interest paid on his mortgage. Finally, there is the matter of inflation; if the inflation rate rose near or above the bond's interest rate during the 15 year holding period then the real rate of return (interest received minus the inflation rate) was marginal at best. If the rate rose above the coupon rate then the real rate of return on the bond was actually negative.

The large increase in real property prices has therefore had a twofold effect upon the housing market. First, during periods of high inflation at least, it has outstripped the return on less risky intangible investments while providing housing at the same time, something a bond obviously cannot do. Second, because of this effect and its actual or imagined consequences in the investor's mind, it can create a heavy demand for mortgage money, especially in times of perceived, future inflationary pressures. The net effect upon building associations, as well as upon other mortgage granting institutions, has been to severely test their ability to provide funds and make a profit at the same time. While this latter generalisation is true for both British and American institutions, the American S&Ls were especially tested during the late 1970s and early 1980s. Somewhat ironically, it was a British method of financing that was ultimately adopted in America in order to cope with the mismatching problem that drove many S&Ls into mergers with others in order to preserve their balance sheets.

ADJUSTABLE AND FIXED RATES

During the 1960s, American commercial banks and savings institutions (both savings banks and S&Ls) were limited on the amount of interest they could pay on deposit accounts. Basically, the various institutions offered the same sort of deposits, or product lines, with one essential difference. Savings institutions were allowed to offer one quarter of 1 per cent more than a commercial bank for a similar sort of account. This was allowed to ensure a continuing deposit base that could be directed into the mortgage market. While this differential provided S&Ls especially with something of a competitive edge, it was the surge in dollar interest rates that made even this small differential obsolete, especially in the face of new financial products that were not hindered by institutional regulations.

The 1970s witnessed a surge of new financial products offering market rates of interest that the traditional depository institutions could not compete with. Prime among them was the money market mutual fund, mentioned in Chapter 2, that offered savers the advantage of a near money market rate on their investment. These funds became more and more popular as interest rates rose and the yield curve actually became inverse. From the saver's point of view, he was able to redirect his savings into current rates while perhaps paying a relatively low rate on his older, fixed rate mortgage. While this situation benefited the saver/investor, it had exactly the opposite effect upon the S&Ls.

While the deposit rates at the S&Ls were fixed, these new instruments began to siphon off funds. This is the process of disintermediation referred to in Chapter 2 and it had a deleterious effect upon S&Ls as well as banks. Between 1978 and 1981, money market funds rose from $10 billion to almost $200 billion outstanding. During the same period, the profit margins of FSLIC insured savings institutions fell from 9.57 per cent (profit) in 1978 to −6.96 per cent (loss) in 1981.[3] And the rate of savings deposits of savings associations began to slow as well. The rate of increase between 1977 and 1978 was 11.4 per cent. Between 1978 and 1979 it fell to 9 per cent and between 1979 and 1980 it was about 8.7 per cent, reaching a low between 1980 and 1981 of only 2.7 per cent. In the following year it finally rebounded to 9 per cent. While short-term interest rates began to recede during the latter years, changes in the regulatory environment also had much to do with the rebounding rate of deposits.

In 1980, Congress passed the Depository Institutions Deregulation and Monetary Control Act. This piece of legislation contained nine titles, several of which directly affected the savings institutions. Specifically, Title 2 provided for the abolition of interest rate ceilings on accounts in institutions covered by the legislation, which included S&Ls. The actual deregulation was completed by the end of March 1986. Equally, Title 4 enabled federally chartered S&Ls to expand consumer lending for loans other than mortgages and issue credit cards as well. But it was the gradual elimination of the amount of interest that could be paid which had the most profound effect upon the S&Ls' funding problems.

The major factor behind these events was not the simple fact that depository institutions were unprofitable but that the old regulatory environment was out of tune with the new highly volatile interest rate environment. In other words, the source of funds was changing rapidly but the uses of funds were much the same as they had been in previous years. Traditionally, the ceiling on deposits meant that the cost of funds to an S&L was given. If mortgage rates on long-term mortgages rose so would the institution's profit margin. So the basic picture was a snapshot frozen in time in favour of the S&L; the only rate that could actually change was the mortgage rate and that only meant enhanced profitability.

The technical snag came when short-term interest rates rose to levels above the long-term mortgage rate that had been traditionally fixed for fifteen or thirty years (a thirty-year fixed rate mortgage is referred to as a 'conventional' mortgage). The profit margin became negative and many S&Ls began losing money because of the inflexibility of the mortgage package. Even when an S&L was able to respond to this phenomenon successfully, its profit margin was still eroded since it no longer had its low interest bearing deposits factored in as a constant source and cost of funds. Assume for a moment that an S&L could take in deposits at 6 per cent and lend them out at perhaps $8\frac{1}{2}$ per cent. It had become accustomed to that sort of spread and had used it in its own internal strategic planning. When the margin was eroded, the association found itself in financial straits.

At the same time, potential home buyers began to shun high interest rate loans because, although tax deductible, the cost of new traditional mortgages at 15 + per cent at the height of the market was difficult to bear. Savings associations responded in part by offering what are known as 'balloon' mortgages; fixed at this high rate initially for perhaps three years and then renegotiated again, hopefully when rates have fallen. But since mortgage rates are not as quick to respond to overall market changes as bonds or financial assets, the borrower was many times still faced with high rates upon renegotiation; in some cases forcing liquidation of the property. A partial solution to the problem was found by deploying adjustable rate mortgages – those changing their periodic interest payments in line with money market rates of interest.

The concept of adjustable rate mortgages was a new innovation to American lending practices although it had been standard practice in Britain for several decades. In the British example, mortgages granted by either commercial banks or building societies for, say, thirty years were subject to periodic changes in the base lending rate. This rate was changed by banks in line with general interest rate trends plus the demand for money. So while the building societies had the flexibility to change the rate on both deposits and mortgages, the homeowner could never predict with any accuracy how many times the rate would effectively change over the life of the loan.

Despite the fact that adjustable or floating rate increases are ultimately borne by the borrower, adjustables did help to keep the British building societies on a fairly even keel during times of interest rate uncertainty. Almost all residential mortgages in the United Kingdom have been granted in this manner. When adjustables were introduced into the United States market their popularity quickly soared.

Adjustables in America are different from their British counterparts in one significant respect. While UK mortgage rates vary with the banks' base rates, American adjustables are granted only with specific interest rate re-fixing periods, speci-fied at the outset. In this manner, they are closely tied to prevalent money market rates.

As an example, a 30-year American mortgage could be tied to the six-month Treasury bill rate. The bill rate becomes the reference rate to which a spread is added. If the spread is 2 per cent, then that amount is added to the bill rate that is itself adjusted to reflect a coupon equivalent yield.[4] This effectively adds more than just 2 per cent to the reference rate. Thus, if the bill rate for 6 months was 10 per cent, the bill would be adjusted to 10.17 and 2 per cent added on top to give an effective rate (quoted on an annual basis) of 12.17 for the first six months. If the bill rate fell to 8 per cent six months later, the second fixing would be 8 per cent, adjusted to 8.11, with 2 per cent again added on top. This would mean that the rate for the first year was an average of the two, 10.14 per cent.

The advantage of this method is that it locks neither lender nor borrower into what may prove to be uneconomical rates of interest for the long-term. In the lender's favour is the fact that a spread can always be guaranteed against the rising cost of funds, now directly tied to short-term interest rates. In the borrower's favour is the ability normally to avoid being locked into a high long-term interest rate for the life of his loan. But to achieve this, he must give up the certainty involved with a fixed rate mortgage. But this does not necessarily mean that the borrower is faced with a potentially limitless mortgage rate, contingent only upon movements in short-term rates.

Most adjustable rate loans have 'caps' and minimum levels of interest rates attached to them. A mortgage with a cap of 15 per cent means that the borrower will never be faced with a periodic payment of more than 15 per cent annual rate. The minimum means that he will never pay less than the rate stipulated. So if the minimum is 9 per cent and rates on the reference instrument should fall below that level, the homeowner will still be locked in at 9 per cent.

The risk implications of this range should be underscored

because it is this concept of rate ranges that have helped S&Ls to healthier balance sheets in recent years. While adjustable rates shift the interest rate risk from the lending institution to the borrower, the lender may still be faced with less of a profit margin than it would have realised under the old regime of fixed deposit rates and fixed rate lending. However, this is a trade-off most mortgage lenders were willing to make in order to remain evenly matched on interest rates paid out as against those received. However, if interest rates exceed 15 per cent in this above example, the lender would again be forced to bear the marginal rise above that rate because the mortgage holder is protected. Conversely, if rates fall below 9 per cent, the mortgage holder would suffer. However, in either case, the total interest rate risk (the difference between the deposit rate given by an S&L and the borrowing rate for new mortgages) has been shifted primarily toward the borrower, with the exceptions just noted. In this respect, American and British mortgage holders share a common financial trait.

The British mortgage holder is less subject to this sort of volatility in time because his rate is not directly tied to a money market rate but to a bank announced rate that is fairly standard for the industry. While the American mortgage holder knows in the example above that he will be subject to sixty 'fixings' over the life of his thirty-year mortgage (two per year, as suggested by the fixing over a six-month Treasury bill) the Briton will never be sure how many changes he will be subject to since the changes in the rates depend upon how many actual changes there are in bank rates and how building societies react to them.

The popularity of adjustables in the United States was quite pronounced when interest rates were high and the periodic changes were cheaper than the traditional mortgage rates. In 1983–4 almost 80 per cent of new American mortgages were granted on an adjustable basis, using many different rates of reference. However, when interest rates began to fall, the trend shifted back to traditionals both as a method of new financing as well as a matter of re-financing outstanding adjustables or high, fixed rate traditionals taken out in preceding years when rates were historically high.

Adjustable rate mortgages helped to restore profitability to many American mortgage originators who had suffered under the old system whereby they were almost automatically mis-

matched under high interest rate regimes. But ultimately, it was
the 1980 Depository Institutions Deregulation and Monetary
Control Act that also played a major role in helping them back
to profitability by enabling them to shirk the old regulations in
favour of a new competitve climate.

NOTES

1. United States League of Savings Institutions, *Source Book*, 1985. The
reason for this reduction was due to both failure of institutions outright
or their amalgamation into larger, more solvent institutions.
2. Ibid. The ability to hold an agency bond or short-term obligation for tax
reasons is one advantage of an American S&L over a British building
society since this particular layer of agency does not exist in Britain.
3. Ibid.
4. The reason that the short-term rate has to be adjusted to a coupon
equivalent is that Treasury bills are quoted on a discounted rate of
interest while most mortgages are quoted on a coupon type rate. Hence
the need for the adjustment.

5 Life Insurance Companies and Pension Funds

Two of the largest types of financial institutions are neither banks nor direct depository institutions. Many times, neither of these will immediately come to mind if the layman is asked to name a large sophisticated financial intermediary. The reason for this lapse is that both institutions devote themselves to a different type of savings and investment function than do banks or building associations. Life insurance companies and pension funds cater to another sort of financial need than do banks that serve as depositories for current needs. Both invest for the individual on a future basis; seeking to protect his future needs for wealth and protection rather than serve more immediate concerns covered by depository institutions.

Although each institution serves a different need and is organisationally and structurally distinct from the other, there is a common denominator between them both in terms of the social welfare benefits provided and, in some cases, a common financial management thread as well. And unlike many other financial intermediaries, this common social welfare function cannot be stressed too heavily. Currently, in the United States and Britain, the state is not able adequately to cover the needs of its elderly or financially distressed, especially if hardship should arise because of the death of the principal wage-earner in a family unit. Regardless of the reasons for this shortcoming, all developed and developing countries above a certain minimal level of wealth have insurance companies and pension funds operating within their economies. Their social role is therefore quite evident, whatever the political ideology; both types of institution afford a certain level of financial assistance above and beyond what the apparatus of the welfare state is able to provide. Without them, the level of poverty as defined as minimal or marginal would be much more widespread among the elderly in many societies, regardless of those societies' national wealth.

Of the two institutions, insurance companies are the older, tracing their origins on both sides of the Atlantic back to the eighteenth century. Pension funds are a more recent phenomenon, developing on a large scale only in the twentieth century. The social reasons for their disparate development can be traced to the industrialisation movement, also originally occurring in the eighteenth century. As more and more of the rural populace moved to urban areas, social welfare practices that had originally been attended to by the extended family, such as care of the elderly, became interrupted by this urban migration and its accompanying breakdown of the large family unit into smaller units searching for wealth in a new, industrialised environment. The social pressures caused by urbanisation required those who could afford protection to provide some level of coverage to maintain their families after the wage-earner's death so that a form of wealth other than transfer of land could be achieved. But it should not be assumed that life insurance companies sprang up immediately with the advent of the industrial revolution. It was to be another hundred years before the modern version of the life insurance company finally began to emerge, offering forms of insurance that appear rather rudimentary today.

Although social and economic developments are usually cited as the main reasons life insurance companies developed, it should also be noted that they could not have emerged successfully unless capital markets were also developing simultaneously so that there was a suitable investment environment in which to seek a rate of return adequate to cover future demands of the newly insured. This, however, will not explain adequately why pension funds were relatively late starters, especially since their function was, and is, to provide funds to the elderly – not simply to leave a lump sum, upon death, to heirs of the wage-earner.

Welfare of the elderly, no longer able to work, was traditionally the role of the family unit, as children provided for their parents until death. This function was simpler when the population remained in one location. But once the population began to grow and become mobile, as in the United States and Britain in the twentieth century, the elderly became a serious problem that only the apparatus of the state was able to cope with. As a result, practical political ideology had to incorporate care of the elderly into its tenets. Regardless of any judgements on how well this end was achieved, the state did construct various programs designed to deal with the increasing demands made by a population that was constantly becoming older, due to improvements in medicine, working conditions, and health and safety legislation. However, parallel developments over the years in the improvements in housing standards, education and in the general standard of living have pushed costs past what the state is able to provide if the elderly are to maintain the standard of living they attained before retirement. Therefore, the role of institutions providing ancillary, or in some cases substitute, services to complement state-provided benefits becomes crucial in continuing social development.

Historical developments and causes aside, insurance companies and pension funds are today among the largest financial institutions on both sides of the Atlantic. The products they offer and the services they provide extend far beyond their original historical prototypes. By virtue of their sheer size, they are also among the largest institutional investors in the capital markets. Besides providing a valuable welfare role, they also provide financial intermediation to specific sectors of the marketplace which in turn aids government funding of debt and also infuses the corporate sector with much-needed debt or equity capital. And they also play a large role in the financial services revolution of the 1980s, although it is the insurance companies that have been the most prominent. The one financial characteristic they both share is their natural preference for long-term financial assets; a factor that distinguishes them from many other financial institutions operating in the marketplace. Their respective portfolio preferences are unique among financial intermediaries because of the unique financial and social roles they perform.

LIFE INSURANCE COMPANIES

Insurance, in some form or other, has been in existence for

centuries, originating in the ancient world. But modern insurance in the Anglo-American tradition traces its origins to the late seventeenth century when Edward Lloyd began the process known as insurance underwriting. Although this original underwriting process was confined to marine insurance, it is nevertheless the origin of all modern underwriting techniques. Lloyd's original spirit is still in active practice today in the London insurance exchange that bears his name.

After marine insurance became popular, insurance quickly adopted other forms. In addition, fire and life companies also sprang up in the seventeenth and eighteenth centuries. The advent of the industrial revolution made life insurance in particular more and more popular. By the end of the American Civil War in 1865, an estimated $600–$700 million worth of life insurance was in force in the United States. Twenty years earlier, the total amount outstanding was less than $5 million. In contrast, some $5 trillion of life insurance was in force at year end 1983 in the United States alone.

This chapter concerns itself exclusively with life insurance because it is the most popular form and because the life companies have a profound impact upon the financial markets. This impact also has implications for the savings and wealth functions because, unlike other specific forms of coverage, life insurance is the only one that is actually used to pass on wealth from individual to individual after death.

TYPES OF LIFE INSURANCE

Before defining the types of life insurance available it should be noted that the various types of policies may be issued to an individual directly or to an individual as a member of a group plan which many times reduces the overall cost of premiums. Group life insurance is ordinarily provided by an employer to its employees as a job related perquisite. The only difference between group and individual insurance is the structure of the policy and the related cost. The group policy can be marginally cheaper because of the lesser aggregate costs of administration to the insurance company undertaking to provide the benefits.

The most popular form of life insurance coverage is referred to as *whole life* insurance, or *straight life*. The name derives from the fact that this type of coverage lasts as long as the individual covered lives and as long as the premiums paid (annual costs to the individual) are not in arrears. The major feature of this type of insurance is the abilitiy of the individual to insure himself for a specific amount of money for a fixed schedule of payments that remain constant over time rather than varying in cost from year to year.

Upon the individual's death, the policy will pay his beneficiaries the insured amount. For instance, assume that an individual originally insured himself for $50 000, paying a premium of $500 per year. Further assume that he lived for forty years after taking out the policy. This means that he paid in $20 000 in premiums during the course of his life. At death, the policy would pay out the $50 000 contracted amount. That is the most obvious feature of whole life insurance. But there are also interim benefits based upon the policy's cash value that also may benefit the policyholder in point in time.

These cash value benefits can be defined as the product of the level premium approach. Because the payments are fixed, those made in the early years of the policy's life are actually higher than the amortised cost of the insurance itself and the excess amount paid in is held in reserve along with any interest earned on the policy. Over time, this reserve will build up, having a stated cash value at any given moment. This cash value has benefits that can be utilised by the policyholder prior to final expiration of the policy. It can be used to borrow against the policy up to the accumulated amount or it may be used as a liquidation value if the policyholder decides to terminate the policy prior to his death.

If the policyholder decides to borrow the cash value of the policy, the interest rate charged on the loan is normally cheaper than commercial borrowing rates. In periods of high interest rates especially, the accumulated cash values can become a cheap source of funds for the individual consumer at the expense of the insurance companies which could obviously obtain a higher rate on the cash in the markets. This phenomenon can also place the company under a liquidity strain if many loans are requested because it otherwise places most of its investment funds in the longer end of the bond market or in the stock market. In short, requests for loans by policyholders place demands for liquidity on the company which it would not otherwise receive under normal conditions. Neither can the insurers adequately predict this sort of demand because it is not part of their usual actuarial calculations.

The other popular form of life insurance is called *term insurance*: coverage lasting for a specified period of time only, not for life. At the end of the stipulated period it ceases, unless renewed. This type of insurance is employed by those requiring coverage, usually for a multiple of their salary, during critical periods of their lives such as their peak earning years. Generally considered, term insurance is the most cost effective of the major life insurance varieties because of the actuarial principles involved. Since it does not last for a lifetime, the expectation is that the individual probably will not die during the period of coverage. While this simple statement seems rather ambiguous, it does illustrate cost effectiveness to the individual and to the insurer. Also, term insurance does not have any cash accumulation benefits and therefore no reserve against the policy so its premiums are not heavily loaded in the early years. They become more expensive toward the end of their specific terms rather than from the outset. So in the early stages, term insurance provides coverage for the least amount of money.

The relative cheapness of term policies has made them a more popular form of insurance over the last thirty years. In 1954, only 16 per cent of ordinary life insurance in the United States, a category including both whole life and term, was classified as term. By the early 1980s, the figure had more than doubled to about 40 per cent of the total amount.[1] This shift, at the expense of whole life, is troublesome for insurance companies because it affects the amount of cash inflows available for longer term investments. As will be noted below, this can deprive insurance companies of funds that they are ordinarily used to receiving. How they deploy the income they do receive will also be affected.

Another form of insurance that has become more and more popular, especially in the United States, where individual retirement plans are more common than they are in Britain, is the annuity. This type pays out death benefits or, if the policyholder is still alive after a certain date, cash benefits to the holder thereafter until his eventual demise. This sort of policy is designed to provide income for those in their later years who lose earning power due to retirement or diminished capacity to work. In this respect, these policies overlap, in a manner of speaking, with benefits provided by pension funds. The major attraction of this sort of plan is that is provides the policyholder with a means of deferring current income tax liability until a future date when the anticipated tax rate will be lower because of the policyholder's age and diminished earning power.

Endowment insurance is another type of insurance more popular in Britain than in the United States. This policy pays its face value when it matures or when the policyholder dies, whichever occurs first. If this latter instance is the case then the beneficiary receives the benefit. In Britain, endowment insurance is often used in conjunction with mortgages, enabling the mortgage holder to pay down the principal and interest on his property while receiving insurance protection at the same time. If the policyholder is alive when the mortgage is paid in full, the policy returns a cash value as well. For this double sort of protection and benefit, the interest rate on endowments is higher than on a traditional British mortgage by about one half of one per cent.

ACTUARIAL CALCULATIONS AND INVESTMENT INCOME

Although it is obvious that insurance is a business with a long-term emphasis, the immediate concern of any life insurance company is the time periods involved in writing an insurance policy. For instance, how long will a person live and how will his premiums be invested? As with any long-term financial calculation, the answer can only be approximated but it nevertheless must be precise enough to match the value of future liabilities with future assets.

When a life insurance company takes on a new policyholder that person must be matched against a demographic profile in order to determine (in general) how long he will live. That particular estimate is based, *inter alia*, upon probability theory, first developed by Pascal and Fermat in the seventeenth century. Combined with more recent developments, insurance companies today are able to arrive at relatively precise actuarial estimates of a particular type of person's life span. As an example, imagine a 35-year-old man applying for $50 000 of whole life insurance. According to current mortality tables published by the American Council of Life Insurance, he has an expected 38.61 more years to live (as opposed to 42.98 for a woman of the same age). In his age bracket, there are recorded 2.11 deaths per 1000 population, on average (as opposed to 1.65 for a woman). On this basis, if the insurance company assumes that he will not surrender his whole life policy, he will be paying premiums for the next thirty-eight years, until his projected death at age 73.61.

Returning to the previous discussion for a moment, if this individual had opted for term insurance instead, his premiums would start to rise after the first year rather than remain fixed. Following the mortality tables, as his life expectancy declines after age 35, his term insurance premiums for, say, ten years would start to rise, illustrating the increasing risk to the insurer. Although it is unlikely that the policy will have to be invoked between the ages of 35 and 45, the risk or possibility of such an occurrence does nevertheless increase. This can be seen in the mortaility tables. At age 45, there is a death rate of 4.55 men per 1000 population; almost double the figure cited for men aged 35. Women aged 45 suffer a mortality rate of 3.56 per thousand, also a 200 per cent increase over age 35.

If one hundred men aged 35 subscribe for whole life insurance then the insurer knows approximately how long they will live and can also calculate standard deviations from the mean as well as make an estimate, using past experience, as to how many will surrender their policies prior to redemption. Once the insurer has these assumptions calculated, it can seek out an investment to adequately cover its needs.

If we further assume that all one hundred men pay the same premium for $50 000 worth of insurance, say $500 per year, then we also know the cash flow of the incoming premiums – $50 000 per year for thirty-eight years. At the end of that time, the company will be faced with payouts of $5 million. In order to ensure that it will have the $5 million on hand, the company needs to find an investment that will give it an adequate return. Most frequently, the investment will be in the bond market or real estate market. The company could also invest in common stocks but would not be assured of a specific return that a fixed income investment can provide.

In both Britain and America, the best long-term investment the insurer will find is a thirty-year government bond, or in the case of the United States, a corporate bond. Although this is technically eight years short of the portfolio length of the liabilities it is the closest the company can come to its maturity needs without assuming undue risk in a lesser quality instrument. Now assume that it takes the first year premiums of the hundred men and invests them in a thirty-year bond paying 12 per cent interest. At the end of the thirty years, the initial $50 000 will be worth $1 500 000, compounded annually at 12 per cent. So while it seems that the insurance company is faced with a large bill in thirty years' time, the reality is that if the premiums for the entire time period are invested at a proper rate the end result is coverage for the insured and profit for the insurer as well.

NATURE OF INSURANCE COMPANY ASSETS

Even from the brief discussion above, it becomes apparent that the amount of coverage and profit an insurance company can provide and obtain depends entirely on both the quality of its asset base and the return it provides. The nature of the assets themselves cover the full spectrum of financial assets, from government and corporate bonds to common and preferred stocks and real estate holdings.

Unlike banks and other depository institutions, life insurance companies do not necessarily need to hold large amounts of short-term money market paper as liquid reserves although they are subject to reserve requirements. This is not to imply that short-term paper will not be held if yield curve conditions dictate. Liquidity to an insurance company means that a portion of its assets must be held in securities that can be easily liquidated, such as government bonds. Other assets such as mortgages or some corporate bonds are bought more for their high yields than for liquidity purposes. The ideal asset mix contains both high yielding financial assets and some real property investments, plus others with lower returns that are easily liquidated, namely government or agency paper.

The reason for emphasising length and yield on an investment rather than liquidity is due to the actuarial projections mentioned above. If the policyholders follow the expected mortality patterns then the only reason a company should need liquidity is if a holder decides to borrow cash against the paid-in value of the policy. Or he could surrender the policy for cash prior to death. In either case, the cash outflow should be adequately covered by the liquid portion of the portfolio, leaving the less liquid, higher yielding portion intact.

The assets of American and British insurance companies in aggregate can be seen in Table 5.1. It should be noted that policy loans – where the policyholder borrows the cash value of the policy – are listed here as assets of the American companies. In the American example, policy loans burgeoned 19 per cent between 1979 and 1980 while overall assets increased by only 11 per cent. This was the period of high American interest rates. Policyholders began to borrow against their policies at a time when insurance company borrowing rates were preferential to those found in the commercial market. While the companies were still able to count these loans as assets, the returns were obviously lower than those found elsewhere.

TABLE 5.1   Assets of American life insurance companies and British insurance companies

	American companies ($ millions)				
			Of which:		
Year	Total amount	Government Securities	Corporate bonds	Equities	Policy loans
1981	525 803	39 502	193 806	47 670	48 706
1982	588 163	55 516	212 772	55 730	52 961
1983	654 948	76 615	232 123	64 868	54 063

	British companies (£ millions)			
			Of which:	
Year	Total amount	Government Securities	Cash	Equities
1981	13 132	3 221	1 096	2 521
1982	16 156	4 257	1 056	3 086
1983	18 641	4 897	1 342	3 725

SOURCES: American Council of Life Insurance, *Fact Book*, 1984; Central Statistical Office, *Financial Statistics*, September 1985

Insurance companies' presence in the financial markets as a whole is considerable. In institutional terms, they rank fourth behind commercial banks, savings and loan associations, and federal loan agencies as a source of funds in the American capital markets, committing $56.5 billion in funds in 1983 alone.[2] While the gross figures are impressive, they do not indicate that, for instance, American life insurance companies are a major source of demand for corporate bonds and equities. While banks and other depository institutions are the primary source of demand for government bonds in the United States, insurers provide substantial demand for corporate obligations because of their need for higher yielding instruments.

Although it is easy to understand how insurance companies use long dated bonds to match their anticipated future payments, bonds are certainly not the only investments of interest, as already mentioned. The need for high yield also leads many companies to invest in the real estate market, the private placement market, and corporate stocks as well. At year end 1983, American life insurers had some $64.87 billion invested in the stock markets (of total assets of $654 billion) while British insurers had £4.5 billion invested in British and overseas stock markets (of a £20 billion). The reason that corporate equities play more of a prominent role in British insurance investments, some 23 per cent as opposed to 10 per cent of American investments, is the historical absence of a corporate, domestic bond market in the United Kingdom over the years since the Second World War. As a result, the highest domestic returns obtainable are found either in corporate equities or UK government bonds, representing 25 per cent of the total invested.

Insurance companies as a whole also represent a considerable source of funds in the British financial markets. At year end 1984, life insurance companies and pension funds combined experienced a net inflow of £16.5 billion.[3] In turnover terms, insurance companies accounted for £11.2 billion in ordinary shares alone, of a total of £40.23 billion on the London Stock Exchange. In other UK company securities, they accounted for £1.66 billion of a total of £3.29 billion and in overseas common shares they accounted for 6.89 billion of 32.6 billion total. The numbers are equally dominant for UK government securities as well.[4]

RESERVES

Life insurance companies, regardless of location, have mandatory policy reserves requirements levelled against them which must be maintained. These reserves are funds set aside in order to meet future obligations to policyholders or their beneficiaries. Although liquidity needs are not as acute as they are for depository institutions this is not to imply that reserves are not necessary. The requirements are set down by the local governmental unit overseeing the area in which they are located or, in the case of Britain, by central government. Unlike bank reserves, insurance company funds of this nature are not used as the focal point of monetary policy but are mainly in place to protect policyholders.

Reserves become doubly important given that many life companies, because of their expertise and ability to create new insurance products, now administer, directly or indirectly, a large number of private pension funds. The close link between the two industries also gives close insight into how individual societies are attempting to come to grips with the problems of a large percentage of their respective populations becoming increasingly older and the demands made upon financial intermediaries as a result.

PENSION FUNDS

The financial services revolution that began in the late 1970s in the United States has had a profound impact upon funding a worker's later years through the use of special funds set aside in addition to the more traditional retirement funds. Prior to that time, most pension funds were organised by employers for their employees, with each making a contribution that was designed to provide for the employee after retirement. But with the advent of deregulation of the financial markets and the rapid acceleration of many new financial products and financial services, pension funds were also directly affected.

Specifically, this set of events has enabled the individual to provide, on a tax deferred basis, for his own retirement in addition to whatever may be provided by an employer. On the face of it, this would not appear to be a particularly revolutionary concept but given the changing social climate and employment patterns of the working population plus newly designed financial instruments catering to a population more prone to early retirement, the impact upon both individual social welfare and financing patterns has been significant. As of this writing, these sorts of plans are only in the early stages in Britain so much of this discussion will be American in orientation.

Although pension funds are a relatively new historical phenomenon, their origins can be traced back to the eighteenth century when soldiers disabled in war were given what would be called today disability pensions. Until the twentieth century, however, most pensions as such were maintained and disbursed by government in both the United States and Britain. Only in the aftermath of the First World War, during the 1930s, did the idea of a government sponsored pension system for all citizens come into effect.

In the United States, old age pensions were inaugurated in 1935 with the founding of the Old Age, Survivors, and Disability Insurance Fund; better known as the social security system. In Britain, the proposals put forth by Lord Beveridge in the 1930s resulted in the adoption of legislation helping to create the modern welfare state that today provides old age and survivors benefits as well as a host of other transfer type payments to the populace. In both cases, workers contribute to a central fund during their working years through a form of withholding tax and, upon retirement or the cessation of work, begin to draw benefits lasting until death.

For the most part, public pension funds such as these plus the numerous others attached to local government or government related agencies or services are not centrally important as financial institutions acting as intermediaries with the financial markets because they are not *funded*; that is, no funds are set aside by the employer or payor prior to the employee's retirement. In an unfunded pension fund, the employer simply agrees to provide benefits for the individual but makes no special financial arrangements in advance. It is the funded pension fund that has the most significant impact upon the financial markets. The funded pension fund is placed in the hands of a trustee whose responsibility is to manage the monies seeking the highest rate of return possible while still protecting the constituents' future benefits. Between the two are partially funded funds that only put aside a portion of money in order to meet future demand.

The reason that a fund must be at least partially funded in order to have an impact as a financial intermediary is that it is those funds set aside by the payor that are invested in the markets. They provide a continual source of demand in the markets, as mentioned in the previous section on insurance companies. Put another way, funded or partially funded funds actively match, or seek to match, anticipated future liabilities with long-term assets. It is the investing process, seeking exponential growth in returns, that provides present demand in the markets in return for a future value that will provide benefits for the constituents of the particular pension plan. But as mentioned earlier in this chapter, the level of benefits provided by governments through their social security plans is not always adequate in providing for the elderly or disabled and that shortcoming has led to the institution of private funds as well. Table 5.2 illustrates public and private coverage.

PRIVATE AND PERSONAL PENSION PLANS

In addition to the government-sponsored public pension funds, employers provide plans as well. This category is known as private pension funds; that is, provided by the private rather than the public sector. While this sort of fund traditionally has provided the bulk of many workers' retirement monies, it has nevertheless also provided problems as well. The most general, but far reaching, has been the matter of portability: many pension plans could not be transferred if an employee decided to change employers. As a response to this problem, personal pension plans came into existence. These schemes allow an individual to fund his own pension plan regardless of where, or for whom, he works.

Personal pension plans in the United States allow an individual to set aside money or securities in a specially designed account in order to accumulate funds for use after a specified age. The maximum amounts that can be sequestered are limited but the tax effects can be significant. For instance, an individual may set aside $2000 per year in an Individual Retirement

TABLE 5.2　Number of persons covered by major pension and retirement programmes in the United States (000 omitted)

	Private plans		Government-administered plans		
Year	With life insurance companies	Other private plans	Railroad retirement	Federal civilian employees	State and local employees
1940	695	3 565	1 349	745	1 552
1945	1 470	5 240	1 846	2 928	2 008
1950	2 755	7 500	1 881	1 872	2 894
1955	4 105	12 290	1 876	2 333	3 927
1960	5 475	17 540	1 654	2 703	5 160
1965	7 040	21 060	1 661	3 114	6 780
1966	7 835	21 710	1 666	3 322	7 210
1967	8 700	22 330	1 641	3 499	7 594
1968	9 155	22 910	1 625	3 565	8 012
1969	9 920	24 410	1 620	3 627	8 303
1970	10 580	25 520	1 633	3 624	8 591
1971	10 880	26 580	1 578	3 596	9 079
1972	11 545	27 400	1 575	3 739	9 563
1973	12 485	28 700	1 582	4 040	9 850
1974	13 335	29 240	1 588	4 057	10 635
1975	15 190	30 300	1 564	4 171	11 230
1976	16 965	na	1 572	4 210	12 290
1977	19 205	na	1 567	4 292	13 124
1978	21 615	na	1 580	4 380	13 400
1979	23 460	na	1 567	4 398	13 680
1980	26 080	na	1 533	4 460	13 950
1981	27 825	na	1 483	4 566	14 230
1982	30 375	na	1 404	4 610	14 504
1983	32 425	na	1 386	4 683	14 524

SOURCES: American Council of Life Insurance, *Fact Book*, 1984

Account (IRA) in any sort of investment he chooses, whether it be bank account, equities, or fixed income securities. The amount actually invested can be taken as a deduction against taxable income in the year invested and any return earned is tax deferred. If a bond placed in an IRA earns 10 per cent interest, then that income is rolled up into a larger amount which is only taxed when the account is liquidated, in the investor's later years. Although the amount that will accumulate will be significantly higher than the amount set aside due to compounding, the eventual proceeds will be taxed as ordinary income in the year of liquidation, at the individual's appropriate tax rate at the time. In theory, that rate should be lower after the individual retires than it was while he was working. So the tax benefit here is in the deferment; the investment is certainly not tax free.

The individual's ability to design such plans plus the marketplace's responses in the form of new, individual type investment products has had a significant impact upon the flow of funds into traditional private pension plans. With the advent of products such as the zero coupon bond and variable rate preferred stock, the individual is now able to achieve growth rates that can either be determined in advance or linked to inflationary growth and money market rates without assuming much risk or excessive portfolio management. More traditional investments, such as corporate equities or fixed rate bonds, have presented a problem to the individual in the past in that their actual growth rates have been difficult to determine in advance. The actual return on an equity can be difficult to determine one year in advance not to mention twenty or thirty years and the actual yield on a bond is also difficult to ascertain because of the rate at which it will actually be compounded. Therefore these new products have been designed to achieve growth for the individual, or any other investor for that matter, while removing some, if not all, of the vagaries surrounding the investment decision.[5]

The personal pension plan thus has added an extra layer of old age protection on top of government and private plans. In a sense, it has been the American government's response to the need to provide as much coverage as possible for the populace through the relaxing of tax measures that would otherwise prove penal. Equally, it has allowed the individual to assume the extra burden, easing pressure from the somewhat frail social security system. The one major drawback to these plans in a pure social welfare sense is that they cannot be taken advantage of by the entire population but only by those who are both in a position to understand the benefits and to utilise them effectively.

INSURED AND NONINSURED PENSION FUNDS

The distinction between funded and nonfunded pension plans is carried one step further organisationally when one considers how the funds are actually administered. Assuming for the moment that funds are either fully, or at least partially, funded, a third party is usually required to administer them. For simplicity's sake, funds shall be categorised here as either insured or noninsured. The former category will also help provide a close link between the insurance industry and pension funds and help destroy the mistaken image that they are two totally distinct businesses.

An insured pension fund is one that is administered by an insurance company. The company itself sets aside funds paid in and creates a policy for those who will retire in the future. Based upon the number of employees expected to retire, the insurance company then establishes a retirement annuity to provide the eventual benefits. How much the annuity will actually provide upon retirement depends upon the assumed rate of return of the investments themselves plus the actual performance of those investments over time.

Within this general process, the structure of the actual annuity policy itself may take different forms. For instance, the annuity may be in the form of a group policy or it may be an individual policy. But in either instance, the method of funding this sort of pension plan provides insurance companies with a substantial amount of business although, in the main, noninsured pension funds still account for more retirement dollars in the United States than do the insured.

Noninsured pension funds, on the other hand, are placed in the hands of a trustee charged with administering them. In many cases, these trustees are the trust departments of commercial banks, legally able to invest in all securities for fiduciary clients. Their methods for achieving growth of the funds will be quite similar to those used by insurers or anyone else faced with future value payments based upon current contributions of cash at prevalent interest rates and stock market expectations.

But it should not be assumed that all trustees are in fact commercial bank trust departments. Employees of the company involved may in fact serve as trustees as can union officials. But in cases such as these, they would still require a financial intermediary to do the actual day-to-day investing for them. If this is in fact the case then the trustees will normally appoint one or more investment advisors to help in the selection of an appropriate portfolio and will also monitor the advisors' performance.

In conclusion, it can be seen that the activities of both life insurance companies and pension funds is of vital importance to a national economy. As the population becomes older, on a yearly basis, due to advances in medicine and science, their importance will continue to grow and their investment decisions will take on an even greater importance as their activities affect greater and greater numbers of people.

NOTES

1. American Council of Life Insurance, *Life Insurance Fact Book*, 1984, p. 25.
2. Ibid., p. 69.
3. Central Statistical Office, *Financial Statistics*, September 1985, p. 72.
4. Ibid., p. 73.
5. Even though many financial products have been developed for personal pension plans, their ultimate performance still depends to a large extent upon the investment decisions made by the individual himself. If tax laws, currently favouring personal plans, should change a substantial effect would be felt both in the financial markets as well as in other sectors of the pension fund and life insurance industries.

6 American Federal Agencies

The basic structure of an international financial agency was introduced in Chapter 1 when the role of development banks and supranational institutions was discussed. The same general process described there, borrowing and guaranteeing funds that are earmarked for a credit worthy borrower of less than the highest calibre, is also practised by domestic agencies on behalf of both institutions and individuals in the United States.

The agency function should not be confused with the role of brokers or investment bankers mentioned in Chapter 3. In the agency sense, the intermediary assumes a liability in the marketplace as a surrogate for another. While depending upon the third party end-borrower for payments so that its own creditors may be satisfied, the agency nevertheless assumes a risk if that third party should default upon payments in point of time. This process is somewhat similar to brokerage or investment banking in that the intermediary also finds itself at risk if the counterparty should fail, but the ultimate distinction between broker and agency lies in the ability of the agency to place its own creditworthiness in place of its end client. This ability is heightened by the fact that these institutions do so for the intermediate to long-term; mostly through the use of public bond borrowings.

As with the case of development banks, this agency function is not well understood because it is a fairly specialised type of financial intermediation that is mostly invisible to the public eye. However, its economic function is vital where practised because it effectively helps centralise the marketplace for borrowers while at the same time shifting the risk of holding debt instruments from institutions to the investing public. This effectively spreads the asset mix of these types of loans to the largest single source of funds available rather than simply relying upon a specialised set of institutions to bear all the risk in a commercial banking sense.

As financial institutions, most government sponsored or directly related agencies do not deal with the general public directly. Their specialised functions preclude them from being direct depository institutions or intermediaries. They are rather providers of funds according to statute and as such rely upon their standing in the credit markets to provide monies to certain sectors of the economy. Nevertheless, their position enables them to be conduits of funds, not receivers of funds from savers. As intermediary institutions, most of them fund themselves by issuing bonds ranging from the short to the long-term and these obligations normally carry a government guaranty. Their government related status make them low risk investments carrying low rates of interest. This security makes them appropriate investments for a wide range of financial institutions already mentioned in this book. As will be seen below, the assistance provided by these agencies ranges from providing funds to the housing market, for student loans, for loans to the agricultural sector, and as import loans to buyers of American goods and services.

THE AGENCY FUNCTION

Agencies are, in a financial sense, the intermediaries' intermediary. They provide funds, or liquidity, to financial institutions by purchasing loans from them, utilising their own standing in the marketplace. While not dealing with the public directly they are nevertheless able to provide funds for specific, and normally 'big ticket', items.

As an example, imagine for a moment an American house-buyer seeking a mortgage for thirty years on a residential dwelling. The potential buyer approaches a bank or other mortgage granting institution and applies for a loan. The institution agrees, sets a rate and releases funds to the buyer. Behind this seemingly simple process, already described in Chapter 4, many more complex factors are at work than may ostensibly meet the eye. The credit process by which the lender decides to grant the mortgage is essentially the same, regardless of locale. But the actual commitment to fund it depends upon the availability of funds and this changes from time to time depending upon the business and interest rate cycle.

Ordinarily, a mortgage originator will fund the long commitment from its pool of deposits, or liabilities. This most often leaves the mortgage institution mismatched because it will not have a captive deposit designated as a thirty-year liability against which it can match the loan, or asset. So the course of interest rates will be of particular concern to the lending institution. If it grants a mortgage at rates deemed appropriate when short-term rates are lower than the long-term lending rates it will make money on the transaction. But if short-term deposit rates begin to rise and exceed the long-term, then the amount of mortgage funds available for future lending may be expected to diminish. This is the liquidity side of the phenomenon already described in Chapter 4.

But if the lender employs one of the direct government or government related agencies it may still be able to provide funds to potential borrowers if the matching factor can be worked out in its favour. The mortgage originator may be able to sell the mortgage to one of the housing finance agencies. When the agency purchases the mortgage, along with others, it effectively provides liquidity to the lending institution through one of several various methods. The net effect is that lenders can continue to originate mortgages, at the same rate or different rates of interest, since the liquidity for the loans is being supplied by the agency/agencies responsible.

On the other side of the coin, the agency raises the money from the marketplace for the purchases of mortgages by issuing debt instruments ranging from the short to the long term. These notes and bonds are a relatively cheap source of funds for the agency for two reasons. First, the agencies themselves are either directly under the auspices of the federal government or closely sponsored by it, as will be seen below. As a result, their respective credit ratings are solid and their debt obligations trade at only a marginal premium to the direct obligations of the Treasury itself. Second, mortgage agencies' obligations are all qualified to be traded equally with government debt for fiduciary institutions, savings and loan associations, and other regulated depository institutions and may be used as collateral at the Treasury itself. There is therefore a sound secondary market behind them and their yields tend to remain low as a result.

Although agencies can package their support for the users of funds in various ways, their function as intermediaries' intermediary remains essentially the same.[1] But with this support comes a form of control as well. They may also affect the actual business of the lender by tightening their own credit criteria. For instance, if a mortgage financing agency decides, for whatever reasons, that it wants to upgrade the types of mortgages it will finance, it may issue tighter guidelines to the mortgage originators. As a result, the originators will be required to tighten their own requirements as well if they hope to continue to sell mortgages to the agency.

The basic agency function also has several important derivative effects, some of which are almost taken for granted in the marketplace but would actually be impossible without both the agency and a developed capital market as well. The first of these is the interest rate factor that enters the borrowing/lending picture because of the agency's institutional presence.

INTEREST RATE STANDARDISATION

The presence of financial agencies providing funds acts as a stabilising factor in the rates of interest charged to the final end-borrower of money. This occurs for two reasons. First, the act of providing liquidity in pools of funds means that only one rate is applied at a given time, with any variations attributed to the lending institution. Second, the presence of the agency operating in the capital markets means that investors will accept a lower rate of interest in return for their investment and this basic rate becomes the benchmark by which borrowing is conducted.

The practical result of the agency function in regard to interest rates can be found in a simple example of a consumer utilising funds. Imagine an individual applying for a loan to be used for higher education or a mortgage. If the lending institution decides to grant the loan, it does so in a manner quite different from the process involved in a corporate loan. The rate of interest charged on the loan will be standard in that it will be the same one charged to all borrowers of similar loans at that point in time. As long as the borrower meets the criteria set down by the lender he will normally be granted the loan. The lender does not qualify him according to credit rating. In other words, if he meets the lender's standards he will be advanced the funds. He does not obtain a preferential rate by exceeding those standards.

In short, this means that all student loans or mortgages granted will be at the same rate until market conditions change. What is unique about this process is that individuals are borrowing at rates not materially higher than those at which the agency itself borrows. This same phenomenon was seen in Chapter 1 as well when the role of development banks was discussed. The agency borrows at its low risk rates and passes on the funds to its constituents (in this case their agents, the lending institutions) that would be less highly rated individually. The difference between the agency rates and those charged to the net borrower reflect administration costs and a small margin of profit. But even if the differential was, say, 3 per cent, it could be strongly argued that the individual is still obtaining money at rates below what the lender might charge on a strictly commercial basis.

Now it may be argued that this standardisation of lending rates can be found in many societies that do not have government agencies providing liquidity to the overall market. And many of these societies did not protect their depository institutions by setting interest rate ceilings on the amount of interest that could be paid to individuals depositing money. But therein lies the ability of those sort of depository institutions to function without the aid of an agency. By allowing both deposit rates and lending rates to vary, the rate of deposit interest varies with the amount charged on loans. Spiralling rates do not do as much damage to the lending institutions' balance sheets as they would when both short-term deposits, with ceilings, and long-term lending rates were fixed.

On the other hand, when interest rates rise in economies without agencies providing liquidity, lenders become wary of lending to individuals especially because of the ultimate fear that the consumer will be unable to service the loan at rates that may continue to rise. Under such conditions, an agency is beneficial because it can continue to provide liquidity for loans, even at high rates, if consumers demand them. This occurs because the ultimate provider of liquidity, the investing public, is attracted to agency obligations with high rates of interest attached. Thus, liquidity continues to be provided if demand exists.

The benefit of the standardisation of lending rates for all consumers of these types of loans means that stability is added to the market which otherwise might dry up partially or fully if rate conditions change substantially. Equally, unless otherwise indicated, the criteria for lending to an individual will not change substantially unless the agency or lender experiences a large number of defaults or non-performing loans. And this standardisation feature also has a practical side effect as well. A lending institution could not realistically grant different borrowers different rates at the same point in time. This would cause an administrative nightmare if fifty individuals borrowed mortgage money in the same week at fifty different rates of interest. Therefore the standard rate is as practical administratively as it is fair to the consumers involved.

AGENCIES AS FINANCIAL STIMULI

In almost all cases, agencies restrict their functions to assisting consumers purchasing selective sorts of capital items or services through institutions. By avoiding direct contact with the end user, they also avoid politicising their institutions. But even using this extreme example serves to underline the true role of agencies in a broader perspective; agencies do not provide direct government subsidies to borrowers but only structural support for a diversified marketplace.

This is true of most American agencies with the possible exception of the Export-Import Bank of the United States. This agency and similar agencies in other countries do provide direct support for importers of their domestically produced goods, normally using the commercial banking system as a conduit. The reasons for considering this form of aid as a form of subsidy will be made clearer in a subsequent section.

Although it is true to say that makers of mortgage, farm, and student loans in the United States benefit from agencies' presence, these organisations' actions are not construed as an indirect form of subsidy. While one of the main benefits may be interest rate standardisation and liquidity, it should not be implied that either are maintained in the face of any or all market conditions. Rates and liquidity are ultimately determined by supply and demand in the market. If lending rates become penal then consumers will find alternate forms of investment or defer borrowing until rates again become attractive. Under such conditions, the agencies' functions will diminish until more advantageous conditions reappear.

So in these cases a distinction must be made between support and subsidy. Most American agencies fall into the former category. While some may argue that providing student loans tied to an agency's position in the market in fact constitutes a subsidy, they should also remember that the intermediary function provided keeps the amount of commercial credit at a lower level than it would be if student loans were financed purely as commercial transactions. This allows banks to free up funds for commercial lending at levels where profitability is greater and default risk lower. And the longer range commercial benefits are also present when considering that a student will be repaying a loan at a rate lower than a bank's rate, enabling him to pay back the principal amount and interest faster and then use future earnings for present and future expenditures rather than servicing a previous debt.

GOVERNMENT SPONSORED AND FEDERAL AGENCIES

Although the term 'agency' has been used here in a general sense for economic and functional purposes, there are in fact two types of agency operating in the United States. The first is the government sponsored agency, an institution that has its capital held by private investors rather than the government itself. The second is an agency directly owned by the government; that is, the capital stock is owned directly by the United States Treasury. While there is no actual difference between them in terms of function, there is a slight interest rate differential on outstanding obligations, favouring direct agencies, meaning that the two can, under similar credit market conditions, vary in yield in the marketplace.

Of the multitude of agencies on both levels, only those with a direct effect on the consumer or those which fit into the generic category discussed in Chapter 1 will be dealt with here. Many agencies' functions are somewhat far removed from the public eye and describing their operations would also require extensive description of the particular environment in which they operate. Only one of these, the Export-Import Bank of the United States, will be mentioned here since this particular agency, and others like it around the world, is truly international in character.

Among the more prominent of the US government sponsored agencies are the Farm Credit System, the Federal National Mortgage Association, the Federal Home Loan Banks, the Student Loan Marketing Association, and the Federal Home Loan Mortgage Corporation. Each organisation is a legally instituted entity with its own independent capital structure, designed to provide specialised financial assistance to different sectors of the domestic economy.

The Farm Credit System is a nationwide system of cooperatively owned banks providing loans and other financial and credit services to the agricultural industry. The system is divided into twelve farm credit districts, each with a Federal Land Bank, a Federal Intermediate Credit Bank, and a Bank for Cooperatives. Each of these three institutions was organised under a different act of Congress and now has a capital structure held by its parallel, constituent organisations on the local level.

On the borrowing and lending level, these institutions do not play a role as depository institutions but simply act as financial intermediaries. If, for example, an agricultural borrower needs a loan, he may apply to one of the several hundred land banks nationwide. As collateral, the loan will be secured by a mortgage on his real property. Since the local land bank has no actual depository base from which the loan can be funded, it must seek funds from the central land bank in its district. The land bank in turn approaches the borrowing arm of the system in New York which provides the money through its own capacity, by borrowing in either the money markets or bond markets.

The matter of sponsorship enters here even though the United States government assumes no on or off balance sheet liabilities regarding the system's external borrowings. Although the institutions at the top of the system are owned by the smaller, constituent members, the banks do operate under federal charter and are supervised by government regulations. Both of these factors account for the agency's historically high standing in the credit markets.

Founded in 1938, the Federal National Mortgage Association, or Fannie Mae as it is known in the market, is one of three agencies specialising in residential mortgages. In 1968, it was split into two distinct entities: a portion remained as Fannie Mae while a new direct federal agency was also established, the Government National Mortgage Association, colloquially known as Ginnie Mae. Today, Fannie Mae is a private institution with shareholders as any other publicly traded company. Its shares trade on the New York Stock Exchange. But unlike the Farm Credit System or Ginnie Mae, no constituent shareholders or the government itself are evident.

Originally, this agency was empowered to provide assistance to the secondary market for federally guaranteed and/or insured mortgages. In 1970, this power was expanded to the non-government loan market, that of the so-called conventional mortgages. Fannie Mae is now authorised to purchase insured and government guaranteed mortgages as well as conventionals. Under its original mandate, the agency made loans to farmers, veterans of the armed services, and others qualifying for government mortgage assistance. The intermediaries were the commercial banks, savings and loan associations, local mortgage agencies, and, in some cases, life insurance companies that originated them.

Conventional mortgages now account for about 55 per cent to 60 per cent of Fannie Mae's purchased portfolio and present a risk to the agency because of the credit risk of an individual mortgage holder not guaranteed by the federal government. In order to mitigate this risk, the agency maintains strict underwriting standards for banks and other mortgage originators and also requires mortgages it purchases to be backed by insurance. By the end of 1984, the total size of Fannie Mae's portfolio of both government sponsored and conventional mortgages was about $78 billion.

In order to finance these mortgage purchases from approved originators, Fannie Mae borrows on the credit markets in its own name. The bulk of its financing is accomplished through the bond market in issues of various maturities. About 80 per cent of its purchases are financed in the bond markets while the balance is borrowed in the money market in issues of up to 360 days to maturity, similar to commercial paper.

As its cousin, Ginnie Mae, Fannie Mae also issues mortgage-backed certificates by which interest and principal pass through from the mortgage holder to the investors purchasing them. Mechanically, the agency acquires the mortgages from the originator, pools them into a package of bonds, guarantees them, and then sells the bonds to the public under its own name. Thus, the payments from the mortgages flow through to the investor holding the agency bonds.

A frequently asked question here centres around the actual ownership of the mortgages. Are they assets of the originating lender, of Fannie Mae, or of the security investor? In fact, they remain assets of the originating lender; they are not agency assets. They remain as assets of the lender which in turn pays guarantee fees to Fannie Mae for its services. Neither is the pass-through security itself a liability of the agency in a direct sense; the investor purchases a part of a pool of mortgages ultimately backed by the agency only in case of default. At year end 1983, about $25 billion of such mortgages was outstanding.

The pass-through security is also used extensively by Ginnie Mae and will be mentioned again below. It is also employed by the Federal Home Loan Mortgage Corporation, or Freddie Mac, which assists members of the Federal Home Loan Banks by providing liquidity to the housing market as well.

The Federal Home Loan Bank, established by an act of Congress in 1932, is organised in much the same way as the Federal Reserve System; that is, it is divided into twelve geographically disbursed regions. Its primary function is to provide credit to the savings and loan industry, if required, in order to ensure an orderly flow of mortgage credit.

The Home Loan Bank Board, overseeing the twelve district banks, provides an analagous service to the Federal Reserve in one particular respect. The Board is responsible for issuing all federal charters for savings and loan associations and mutual savings banks in much the same way that the Fed does for federally chartered commercial banks. About 3500 institutions are currently members of the system. Basically, each institution opting for membership must purchase capital in its own local district bank in a specific proportion related to the unpaid principal on its outstanding mortgage loans.

The Home Loan Bank borrows in the marketplace through both bond and discount note issues in order to provide system liquidity. The maximum maturity for its bonds is usually ten years. This differentiates it from the other mortgage assistance agencies that often borrow for as long as thirty years in order to match conventional mortgages. One of them is Freddie Mac, an agency sometimes confused with the Home Loan Bank because of the similarity of names and, to an extent, of function as well.

The Federal Home Loan Mortgage Corporation was established in 1970 to maintain the availability of (mostly) residential mortgage credits by purchasing loans from originators. It purchases both conventional and federally assisted mortgages, with the former accounting for over 95 per cent of its portfolio.

Freddie Mac is owned by the twelve Federal Home Loan Banks who hold its capital stock and it also shares an interlocking board of directors with the Home Loan Banks. However, its debt obligations are distinct from those of the Home Loan Bank. Freddie Mac's range of borrowing is somewhat broader than that of its parent organisation. Basically, its funding comes from three different sources: the issuance of mortgage participation certificates, collateralised mortgage obligations, and guaranteed mortgage certificates in addition to a discount note program.

A mortgage participation certificate represents an interest in either a conventional or federally guaranteed mortgage previously purchased by the agency. Every month each bondholder receives a prorated share of both principal and interest payments collected on mortgages in the pool. The agency guarantees the payment of both. Originally, most of the mortgages involved were issued as thirty-year instruments, as were the participation certificates, although in reality both are assumed to have an average life of about twelve years due to early prepayments. Most importantly, because these obligations are secured by real property they are able to be purchased by thrift institutions and considered as real property loans for tax purposes.

A collateralised mortgage obligation is a general obligation of Freddie Mac secured by a pool of conventional mortgages owned by the agency. In this respect, they are first mortgage bonds, backed by assets rather than simply by full faith and credit guarantees. Guaranteed mortgage certificates are securities representing individual interest in conventional residential mortgages purchased by Freddie Mac. They repay principal annually and interest semi-annually.

The pass-through concept, employed by Fannie Mae and Freddie Mac, is probably the best example of an intermediary instrument spanning the bridge between mortgage borrower, lending institution, agency, and the investing public. It is also successfully employed by Ginnie Mae, a direct government agency. But before discussing it, the last of the government sponsored agencies will be examined.

The last of the government sponsored agencies dealt with here is the Student Loan Marketing Association, known in the marketplace as Sallie Mae. This agency is one of the newest, established by the Higher Education Act of 1965. Although Sallie Mae's activities have become well known and accepted in the United States, its importance in a comparative sense has occasionally been the focus of attention in Britain as well, especially as Conservative governments seek alternatives to direct state aid for students in institutions of higher learning. Sallie Mae necessarily then becomes an agency requiring some scrutiny because its sole function is to make higher education loans available to those requiring them in much the same way that mortgage agencies make housing funds available.

Sallie Mae is a stockholder-owned corporation mandated to provide liquidity for banks and other institutions engaged in federally guaranteed loan programs for students. The lending institution provides the funds to the applicant and the loans are either directly insured or reinsured by the United States government. Funds are provided either by purchasing loans or offering advances to eligible institutional lenders. In some cases, especially if a general liquidity shortage exists, this agency can lend directly to, or act as a source of funds to lenders in turn.

As other sponsored agencies, Sallie Mae finances its activities by the sale of debt securities. The one difference between Sallie and the other agencies already mentioned is that the Association (to date) offers only variable rate securities to the investing public, not fixed rate debt. It sells short-term discount notes to the public and most recently began offering short-term floating rate notes as well.[2]

Although this chapter has only dealt with certain American sponsored and direct agencies, the full range of the agencies and their activities can be found in Table 6.1. Direct government agencies differ slightly, if at all, from the sponsored variety. Usually, the power of the federal agency is broader and may provide a direct guaranty of government itself. The real difference between them, and particularly in the securities they issue,

TABLE 6.1   Direct and sponsored agencies of the United States Government*

Agency	General purpose
Federal Financing Bank	Consolidate government cost of financing
Farm Credit System	Loans, etc., to agricultural sector
Federal Home Loan Banks	Provides liquidity to thrift industry
Federal Home Loan Mortgage Corporation	Provides liquidity for residential housing
Federal National Mortgage Association	Provides liquidity to housing market
Student Loan Marketing Association	Provides liquidity for student loans
United States Postal Service	Borrows to provide mail service
Federal Housing Administration	Improve housing standards and conditions
Government National Mortgage Association	Provides liquidity to housing market
Export-Import Bank of the United States	Finances exports and imports
Farmers Home Administration	Rural farm loans and homes
General Services Administration	Management of government property
Maritime Administration	Ship mortgages
Small Business Administration	Assistance to small businesses
Tennessee Valley Authority	Provides power to Tennessee River area
Washington Area Metropolitan Area Transit Authority	Mass transit in Washington, DC

*That had or do have securities outstanding
SOURCE: First Boston Corporation, *Handbook of Securities of the United States Government & Federal Agencies*, 1984

is found not in a functional sense but in a financial one as already mentioned. The marketplace places a marginally higher value on the obligations of a direct agency because they represent directly guaranteed obligations of the government itself whereas the sponsored agencies' debt is indirectly guaranteed. But in the former case it should be noted again that agency debt is not that of the Treasury itself but of an institution owned by the Treasury.

Of all of the federal agencies, only three will be discussed here, the Federal Housing Administration, the Government National Mortgage Association, and the Export-Import Bank of the United States. The six others are of no less importance but their impact as financial institutions operating in the marketplace is somewhat limited and will be omitted here.

The Federal Housing Administration (FHA) is an agency better known in the retail marketplace than in the financial markets where its borrowings are quite small when compared to those of other agencies. Specifically, the FHA is mandated to encourage house building by providing mortgage insurance to both builders and buyers of homes as well as to mortgage lenders. Most FHA insurance is designed to ensure that funds are provided to buyers of residences. But it does not actually make loans nor does it build houses; its sole function is to encourage residential housing. For the insurance it provides it receives fees and premiums in return.

Ginnie Mae is, on the other hand, much better known in the marketplace than it is to potential home buyers on the retail side. Ginnie Mae was established in 1968 when Fannie Mae was rechartered as a private corporation. This particular agency was established as a government corporation within the Department of Housing and Urban Development to administer mortgage support programs.

The major activity of this agency lies in its mortgage backed securities program which has aided in the development of the nation's secondary mortgage market. The mortgage backed securities program serves as a conduit between the residential mortgage market (as borrowers) and the bond markets (as lenders). In this manner, it provides a similar function to Fannie Mae and Freddie Mac.

The most popular bond issue of the Association is the pass-through certificate. A mortgage originator sells a pool of mortgages to Ginnie Mae which in turn packages it as its own security and sells it into the market. The agency guarantees timely payments of interest and principal. Unlike US government securities, the interest (and principal repayments) are paid out monthly, thus providing the investor with a relatively high yield because of the monthly compounding factor used in the yield calculations.

If the mortgage holder should default on his payments then the agency will pick up the shortfall, providing the government agency guaranty. Because of these two major attractions, Ginnie Mae has become a well accepted borrower in the bond markets with an estimated $160 billion in outstanding securities at year end 1983.

The attractiveness of Ginnie Mae securities can also be found in the financial futures market where a thirty-year future exists on the agency's long-term obligations. As of this writing, it is one of the few non-government debt issues having a future trading with it. However, it should be noted that because of the monthly payments factor plus the short average life that also characterises Fannie Mae obligations, it has not become as popular a futures instrument as the more traditional Treasury bond future.[3]

Several times earlier in this chapter it was mentioned that agency issues trade at a slight yield premium to US Treasury issues even though they have the backing of the government. This occurs not because the market is necessarily sceptical of them but it does nevertheless attach a default risk premium to the issues. In the unlikely event of a default by a direct agency, the Treasury would undoubtedly pay full interest and principal to bondholders but the amount of time necessary to do so would mean opportunity losses to the investors. As a result, the marketplace demands a slight premium in yield and this small spread over comparable Treasury issues is accepted by both borrower and investor alike.

The last of the agencies to be discussed here is no longer a frequent borrower in the bond markets. The Export-Import Bank of the United States (Eximbank) was created in 1934 and currently functions under legislation instituted in 1945. Originally, the Eximbank was established to facilitate trade with the Soviet Union, but today has expanded its horizons universally. Its purpose is to aid in the financing of exports by granting loans, export credit insurance, and guarantees. Although it is supposed to finance both exports *and* imports, the former is the real focus of its activities.

This agency spurs exports by granting loans in US dollars to the foreign importer of domestic goods. It can also grant export credit insurance by insuring the domestic producer against its foreign counterparty defaulting on the amount due for various reasons, whether they be commercial risk, political risks, or a combination of the two that hinder payment.[4]

Loans made to foreign purchasers of American goods extended by the Eximbank take several forms. For instance, the bank may fund up to 50 per cent of a purchase of an American good at a subsidised rate of interest while requiring the importer's bank to finance the balance. Repayments on such loans tend to extend as long as five years. Alternatively, the bank provides discount loan programmes of up to five years in maturity at approximately one per cent less than commercial banking rates.

In a very general sense, the Eximbank is one of the few financial institutions that must actually take into account the state of the American economy in an international perspective as it makes or changes policy. For instance, the bank must calculate any adverse effects of its activities on the US balance of payments. For this reason, it and similar institutions around the world are more concerned with financing exports from the country rather than imports to it. While this may superficially appear to be lacking in economic importance, it should also be kept in mind that extreme competitiveness from agencies of this sort, seeking to further their countries' export positions, can have knock-on effects by enhancing international competitiveness to the point where their countries may actually be hurt in the longer run by others who seek to be equally or more competitive. And the sorts of exports it finances can also come under close political scrutiny at times from both home and abroad.

Regardless of interpretation, the Eximbank's major purpose is to stimulate trade by providing select foreign buyers with US dollars. And also worthy of mention is the fact that it uses the commercial banking system, both in the United States and abroad, as the conduits for funds. In short, it works with its clients' commercial banks to arrange loan facilities, subsidy-type programs, and means for repayment. In these practical cases, it acts behind the scenes in a similar fashion to the mortgage assistance agencies: it deals with banks in the first instance rather than the end client.

As mentioned, the Eximbank is no longer a familiar visitor to the bond and money markets. Until 1973, it issued bonds but since that time has relied upon the Federal Financing Bank (see Table 6.1) as its major source of medium term funds. The bank's capital stock is held solely by the United States Treasury and it has the authority to borrow $5 billion in additional funds if necessary. It has not had to tap that extra line of capital because of a large surplus of retained earnings, currently totalling about $2 billion.

AGENCY BORROWING LIMITS

Each federal and government sponsored agency, with the exception of the Eximbank, currently has access to the debt markets but not without internally imposed limits. Although it is tempting to think that these agencies have unrestricted borrowing power, they are all actually restricted in the amount of money they can borrow. The amount of debt incurred must be in a specific proportion to the amount of capital stock paid in. For instance, Fannie Mae is restricted to borrowing no more than thirty times the sum of its capital and surplus. In this respect, United States agencies also share a trait with other international supranationals and lending agencies. This borrowing ceiling is designed to ensure that the institution does not overextend itself in the marketplace only to later find its capital base and reserves insufficient to cover any future, unforeseen exigencies. The only way that the borrowing level may be increased prudently is to increase the amount of paid-in capital from the shareholder/shareholders. The debt outstanding of federal and federally sponsored agencies in aggregate can be found in Table 6.2.

In conclusion, the agency function can be seen as a broad activity that affects many sectors of the American domestic economy. Given the size and diversity of the economy, agencies help in standardising borrowing and lending practices that might otherwise vary from geographic region to region, based

TABLE 6.2 Outstanding debt of United States federal and federally sponsored agencies

Agency	1982	1983	1984	1985				
				Aug.	Sept.	Oct.	Nov.	Dec.
FEDERAL AND FEDERALLY SPONSORED AGENCIES	237 787	240 068	271 220	289 277	288 657	292 584	293 930	293 905
Federal agencies	33 055	33 940	35 145	35 338	35 903	35 990	36 121	36 390
Defense Department	354	243	142	89	82	79	75	71
Export-Import Bank	14 218	14 853	15 882	15 744	15 419	15 417	15 417	15 678
Federal Housing Administration	288	194	133	116	117	116	115	115
Government National Mortgage Association participation certificates	2 165	2 165	2 165	2 165	2 165	2 165	2 165	2 165
Postal Service	1 471	1 404	1 337	970	1 940	1 940	1 940	1 940
Tennessee Valley Authority	14 365	14 970	15 435	16 180	16 106	16 199	16 335	16 347
United States Railway Association	194	111	51	74	74	74	74	74
Federally sponsored agencies	204 732	206 128	236 075	253 939	252 754	256 594	257 809	257 515
Federal Home Loan Banks	55 967	48 930	65 085	71 949	72 384	73 260	73 840	74 447
Federal Home Loan Mortgage Corporation	4 524	6 793	10 270	13 393	12 720	13 239	11 016	11 926
Federal National Mortgage Association	70 052	74 594	83 720	91 318	91 693	92 578	94 576	93 896
Farm Credit Banks	73 004	72 816	71 193	70 092	68 287	69 274	69 933	68 851
Student Loan Marketing Association	2 293	3 402	5 745	7 187	7 670	8 243	8 444	8 395
FEDERAL FINANCING BANK DEBT	126 424	135 791	145 217	152 941	153 513	153 565	154 226	153 373
Lending to federal and federally sponsored agencies								
Export-Import Bank	14 177	14 789	15 852	15 729	15 409	15 409	15 409	15 670
Postal Service	1 221	1 154	1 087	720	1 690	1 690	1 690	1 690
Student Loan Marketing Association	5 000	5 000	5 000	5 000	5 000	5 000	5 000	5 000
Tennessee Valley Authority	12 640	13 254	13 710	14 455	14 381	14 474	14 610	14 622
United States Railway Association	194	111	51	74	74	74	74	74
Other Lending								
Farmers Home Administration	53 261	55 266	58 971	63 779	64 169	63 969	64 189	64 234
Rural Electrification Administration	17 157	19 766	20 693	21 463	21 676	21 792	21 826	20 654
Other	22 774	26 460	29 853	31 721	31 114	31 157	31 428	31 429

SOURCE: *Federal Reserve Bulletin*, May 1986

upon local economic factors. Through their operations, borrowers can find funds available that might otherwise be unobtainable. But in almost all cases, liquidity is provided only if the end borrower is creditworthy in his own right.

NOTES

1. Whether agencies be American or international in character they all use the commercial banking system in their respective countries or geographic areas as the intermediary between themselves and the third party whom they will ultimately serve.
2. In this case, the floating rate instrument pays an interest rate of 125 basis points, or 1.25 per cent over the rate on 91-day US Treasury bills.
3. For a further explanation see Brendan Brown and Charles R. Geisst, *Financial Futures Markets* (London: Macmillan; New York: St Martin's Press, 1983), especially Chapter 4.
4. Insuring commercial and political risks in the United States in order to protect exporters is also done by the Foreign Credit Insurance Association, a consortium of private insurance companies working in conjunction with the Eximbank.

Conclusion

In periods of rapid change, writing descriptions of financial institutions and their functions can be especially difficult. This has always been true of specialised financial books but now it is becoming equally true for the more general type of survey. Even within the general format of this present volume, no less than four different cross-currents have recently occurred making generalisations more and more difficult.

For example, large American credit companies, some attached to capital goods manufacturers, have been heavily involved in granting short-term business loans; a function long attached solely to commercial banks. Insurance companies have, in some cases, entered the real estate market by making mortgage loans. American commercial banks, through their London branches and subsidiaries, have entered the British mortgage market by using their presence in the international capital markets to raise sterling for lending. And many pension funds have invested in works of art for their portfolios – the type of investment that bears no distinguishable rate of return until it is eventually sold.

In these examples, and in many others, it can be seen that the financial services revolution has indeed allowed, as well as forced, many traditional institutions to change their stripes in order to survive. This general undercurrent has been evident in each chapter. However, as financial institutions in both Britain and America become more 'internationalised', helping to chip away at domestic regulations, a counter-trend is also developing aimed at tightening controls over these new all-service institutions, especially if a commercial bank is involved.

In this latter instance, financial innovation should not be confused with lack of regulation. The experiences with international lending in the late 1970s and early 1980s alone have

121

proved that even generally accepted banking practices can be overlooked in the unregulated international arena. A surfeit of loanable dollars and no small number of borrowers led many commercial banks to skew their loan portfolios towards the developing world in search of higher profit margins in order to bolster sagging domestic profitability. This sort of excess has shown that, while banks may require more varied ways to make money in order to weather different types of economic and business cycles, they must still be controlled in their activities. In the wake of the international debt crisis, a powerful school of thought has emerged that now considers commercial banks to be public utilities and would regulate them in much the same way as any other institution providing basic services to the community.

The financial services revolution has one overriding central issue yet to be resolved. Simply stated, what is, and will be, the structure and functions of a commercial bank in the future? In the United States, the envisioned model seems to be the European-style 'universal bank', performing commercial, investment and trust banking under one roof. In Britain, the same model also emerges, but a consolidation movement among the clearing banks seems to be taking place in the first instance. The final product, some years away, will probably be an institution that could dominate the domestic economy in much the same way that the large West German and Swiss banks dominate theirs. The taking of deposits, granting of loans, issuance of securities and investing of funds on a fiduciary basis will ultimately be performed by one type of institution currently called a 'commercial bank'.

Although the movement certainly has momentum, it would be a mistake to assume that these new financial institutions will be able to operate in a regulation-free environment simply because they helped destroy the older regulatory climate. To allow them to do so would be a return to the excesses of the past that created, *inter alia*, the Wall Street crash of 1929 and the international debt problems of the 1980s. But before any new regulatory environments can be created, the older must be allowed to pass out of existence. The 'Big Bang' in Britain and the move toward inter-state banking in the United States are just two examples of this movement.

Index